Writing Program Administration

Journal of the Council of Writing

Editors
Tracy Ann Morse .... East Carolina University
Patti Poblete .... South Puget Sound Community College
Wendy Sharer .... East Carolina University

Book Review Editor
Kelly Moreland .... Minnesota State University, Mankato

Assistant Editor
Mina Bikmohammadi .... East Carolina University

Editorial Board
Nancy Bou Ayash .... University of Washington
David Blakesley .... Clemson University
Beth Brunk .... University of Texas at El Paso
Sheila Carter-Tod .... University of Denver
Sherri Craig .... Virginia Tech University
Wonderful Faison .... Jackson State University
Collie Fulford .... University at Buffalo
David Green .... Howard University
Teresa Grettano .... University of Scranton
Sarah Z. Johnson .... Madison College
Erin Lehman .... Ivy Tech Community College
Alexandria Lockett .... Spelman College
Staci Perryman-Clark .... Western Michigan University
Darci Thoune .... University of Wisconsin–LaCrosse
Amy Vidali .... University of California, Santa Cruz

Production and distribution of *WPA: Writing Program Administration* is managed by Parlor Press.

Land Acknowledgment: We acknowledge that much of the work of *WPA: Writing Program Administration* is done on the traditional lands of the Tuscarora People, the Steh-Chass band of the Squaxin Island Tribe and Nisqually Indian Tribe, the Dakota Nation, the Cherokee People, and other Indigenous Peoples. While the work of a journal is multivocal, collaborative, and now often virtual, we believe it is important to recognize that each participant labors within space that was often unceded by its ancestral peoples. We do this to reaffirm our commitment and responsibility to mindful and equitable scholarship. We also invite you to review the list of resources used to craft this statement on the WPA website.

Council of Writing Program Administrators

Executive Board

Kelly Blewett, President .... Indiana University East
Erin Lehman, Vice President .... Ivy Tech Community College of Indiana
Lilian Mina, Past President .... University of Alabama at Birmingham
Jacob Babb .... Appalachian State University
Daryl Lynn Dance .... Hampton University
Talisha Haltiwanger Morrison .... University of Oklahoma
Michelle Bachelor Robinson .... Spelman College
Mary Lourdes Silva .... Ithaca College
Darci Thoune .... University of Wisconsin-La Crosse

Ex Officio Members

Christal Seahorn, Treasurer .... University of Houston-Clear Lake
Amanda Presswood, Secretary .... Hope College
Doug Hesse, Archivist .... University of Denver
Michael Pemberton, Director, CES .... Georgia Southern University
Jonikka Charlton, Assoc. Dir., CES .... University of Texas, Rio Grande Valley
Tracy Ann Morse, Co-editor, *WPA* .... East Carolina University
Patti Poblete, Co-editor, *WPA* .... South Puget Sound Community College
Wendy Sharer, Co-editor, *WPA* .... East Carolina University

Guide for Authors

WPA: Writing Program Administration publishes empirical and theoretical research on issues in writing program administration. We publish a wide range of research in various formats, research that not only helps both titled and untitled administrators of writing programs do their jobs, but also helps our discipline advance academically, institutionally, and nationally.

Possible topics of interest include:

- writing faculty professional development
- writing program creation and design
- uses for national learning outcomes and statements that impact writing programs
- classroom research studies
- labor conditions: material, practical, fiscal
- WAC/WID/WC/CAC (or other sites of communication/writing in academic settings)
- writing centers and writing center studies
- teaching writing with electronic texts (multimodality) and teaching in digital spaces
- theory, practice, and philosophy of writing program administration
- outreach and advocacy
- curriculum development
- writing program assessment
- WPA history and historical work
- national and regional trends in education and their impact on WPA work
- issues of professional advancement and writing program administration
- diversity and WPA work
- writing programs in a variety of educational locations (SLACs, HBCUs, two-year colleges, Hispanic schools, non-traditional schools, dual credit or concurrent enrollment programs, prison writing programs)
- interdisciplinary work that informs WPA practices

This list is meant to be suggestive, not exhaustive. Contributions must be appropriate to the interests and concerns of the journal and its readership. The editors welcome empirical research (quantitative as well as qualitative), historical research, and theoretical, essayistic, and practical pieces.

Submission Guidelines

Please check the *WPA* website for complete submissions guidelines and to download the required coversheet. In general, submissions should:

- article submissions should be a maximum of 7,500 words. Submissions for the "Everything Is Praxis" section should be a maximum of 5,000 words. Please see the WPA website for full details on submitting to the "Everything Is Praxis" section.

- be styled according to either the *MLA Handbook* (9th edition) or the *Publication Manual of the American Psychological Association* (7th edition), as appropriate to the nature of your research;
- include an abstract (maximum 200 words);
- contain no identifying information;
- be submitted as a .doc or .docx format file; and
- use tables, notes, figures, and appendices sparingly and judiciously.

Submissions that do not follow these guidelines or that are missing the cover page will be returned to authors before review.

Reviews

WPA:Writing Program Administration publishes both review essays of multiple books and reviews of individual books related to writing programs and their administration. If you are interested in reviewing texts or recommending books for possible review, please contact the book review editor at wpabookreviews@gmail.com.

Announcements and Calls

Relevant announcements and calls for papers may be published as space permits. Announcements should not exceed 500 words, and calls for proposals or participation should not exceed 1,000 words. Submission deadlines in calls should be no sooner than January 1 for the fall issue and June 1 for the spring issue. Please email your calls and announcements to wpaeditors@gmail.com and include the text in both the body of the message and as a .doc or .docx attachment.

Correspondence

Correspondence relating to the journal, submissions, or editorial issues should be sent to wpaeditors@gmail.com.

Subscriptions

WPA: Writing Program Administration is published twice per year—fall and spring—by the Council of Writing Program Administrators. Members of the council receive a subscription to the journal and access to the *WPA* archives as part of their membership. Join the council at http://wpacouncil.org. Information about library subscriptions is available at http://wpacouncil.org/aws/CWPA/pt/sp/journal-subscriptions.

Writing Program Administration

Journal of the
Council of Writing Program Administrators
Volume 48.12 (Fall 2024)

Contents

Editors' Introduction: Seeking the Next Editor(s) for WPA 7
    Tracy Ann Morse, Patti Poblete, Wendy Sharer, and
    Kelly Moreland

Everything Is Praxis

Overenrolled for the Summer: Graduate Instructor Labor,
Course Caps, and Other Compounding Impacts 12
    Gavin P. Johnson, Yu Lei, Rachel McShane,
    Haomei Meng, Reza Panahi, and Gouda Taha

FAQ: Developing & Maintaining Shared Curriculum 30
    Mariya Tseptsura and Rochelle Rodrigo

Essays

Using a Faculty Survey to Model Successful Instruction in
First-Year Writing: Faculty Development
Without Faculty Conflict..47
    Liberty Kohn

Designing DSP: UX and the Experience of Online Students 69
    Kathleen Kryger and Catrina Mitchum

Building Effective Arguments about Writing Class Size and
Workload 89
    Todd Ruecker and Galen Gorelangton

Are We Preparing Students to Write across the Curriculum?:
An Analysis of Learning Outcomes for First-Year Composition
at Two-Year Colleges.. 110
    Teresa Thonney

Book Reviews

A Transdisciplinary Approach to Writing Knowledge Transfer: Applications in Teaching and Research 130
    Hunter Little

Review of *Two-Year College Writing Studies* 138
    Donny Penner

Editors' Introduction: Seeking the Next Editor(s) for WPA

Tracy Ann Morse, Patti Poblete, Wendy Sharer, and Kelly Moreland

Before we introduce you to the outstanding articles in this issue, we want to alert you to an exciting opportunity: CWPA is looking for the next editor or editorial team for *WPA: Writing Program Administration*! Our term as the editorial team will end with issue 49.2, spring 2026, and we are excited to be part of the committee that will identify the person or persons to carry forward the important work of the journal. Full details are below. Please consider applying!

Call for the Next Editor/Editorial Team for
WPA: Writing Program Administration
The Council of Writing Program Administrators is seeking the next editor or editorial team for its journal, *WPA: Writing Program Administration*. The term is for three years, with possibility for a two-year renewal. Our current editorial team of Tracy Ann Morse, Patti Poblete, and Wendy Sharer will conclude their term with the spring 2026 (49.2) issue.

The new editor or editorial team will work with the current team to publish content already in development and process submissions in fall 2025 and spring 2026, and assume full responsibility for content and production beginning with the fall 2026 (50.1) issue.

Interested applicants should have the following qualifications: publications and expertise in the field of writing program administration and related areas; knowledge of the issues that have preoccupied the field, both historically and in the recent past; familiarity with the journal, an understanding of the role the journal plays in the field and a vision for the journal's future; a commitment to diversity and inclusive editorial practices; current membership in and a history of involvement with CWPA; strong editorial and organizational skills; and prior editorial and reviewing experience.

We especially encourage applications from marginalized and underrepresented scholars and prospective editorial teams.

To apply, please submit an application letter explaining why you are qualified for this position and describing any resources or support your institution(s) will be able to provide (released time, clerical support, startup funds, etc.), as well as resources you will request from CWPA. Applicants should also submit a current CV for each member of the prospective editorial team. If you are proposing an editorial team, please explain how you will work together on editing and production of the journal. Upon request, additional information about editorial responsibilities and workflow, journal finances, and production timelines will be made available to prospective editors. Address queries to Jacob Babb, Chair of the Publications Committee, at babbjs@appstate.edu.

Send the application electronically as a single file to Jacob Babb at babbjs@appstate.edu.

Application Deadline: **February 15, 2025**. Members of the Publications Committee will review materials and select applicants to invite for virtual interviews to be held in March 2025. We hope to finalize an agreement with the new editor or editorial team no later than May 15, 2025.

In This Issue

Everything Is Praxis

Thre will perhaps never be a composition class that operates within perfect conditions, and "Overenrolled for the Summer: Graduate Instructor Labor, Course Caps, and Other Compounding Impacts" quite starkly illustrates how the intersections of the un-ideal can quickly and exponentially exacerbate the challenges that instructors face. Particularly, Gavin P. Johnson, Yu Lei, Rachel McShane, Haomei Meng, Reza Panahi, and Gouda Taha chronicle how they, a group of graduate students and a WPA, succeeded—but struggled—through a five-week summer session of courses. What happens, after all, when you're teaching a class in half the time you usually do and enrollment exceeds the recommended course cap? What do you do if you're also a graduate student taking classes yourself, and labor conditions and even residential constraints mean you aren't materially secure? If you're the WPA, how do you maintain a pedagogically sound and professionally supportive program? The authors of "Overenrolled for the Summer" invite us to join their conversation and suggest actionable steps that administrators can take to advocate and strengthen their programs.

The genre Mariya Tsepstura and Shelley Rodrigo have chosen for their "Everything is Praxis" piece enhances the applicability of what they share. "FAQ: Developing & Maintaining Shared Curriculum" provides essential questions for WPAs to consider at different points along the lifespan of program-wide use of common outcomes, syllabi, textbooks, assignments, LMS course shells, and other components of "shared curriculum" that are designed to support a writing program and its people. Beginning with considerations of the need (or lack thereof) for a shared curriculum, Tsepstura and Rodrigo prompt readers to identify and involve writing program stakeholders throughout the processes of curriculum development, promotion, implementation, maintenance, assessment, and revision. The generative questions guiding the FAQ are each followed by specific suggestions and examples of how WPAs might respond in light of their local institutional contexts.

Essays

Many small or medium English departments find that their tenure-line faculty teach the majority of first-year writing classes, sometimes autonomously. When this is the case, first-year writing instruction and curriculum can be varied and incohesive. In "Using a Faculty Survey to Model Successful Instruction in First-Year Writing: Faculty Development Without Faculty Conflict," Liberty Kohn explores the results of studying his department's first-year writing praxis. Kohn surveyed his colleagues (not as a WPA, they don't have one at his school) to inform assessment and professional development. In this article, Kohn shares that he was able to discuss the results of the survey with his department. He highlights the similarities in their assignments and process-based pedagogy and explains how he used bar graphs to visually present some of the areas they differed in. By navigating discussions that highlighted some of the stronger teaching practices that not many faculty engaged in, Kohn persuaded his colleagues to shift some of their first-year writing pedagogy. Kohn encourages WPAs to use a survey of their faculty who were trained in different disciplines and teach first-year writing as a way to have discussions about praxis and inform assessment.

Much has (rightly) been made of the inequities that placement practices have historically replicated in writing programs, and still more ink has been devoted to various ways institutions have attempted to address those flaws. One of those methods, directed self-placement (DSP), has become increasingly popular as of late, but colleges are still struggling to establish its efficacy. In "Designing DSP: UX and the Experience of Online Students," Kathleen Kryger and Catrina Mitchum pose the question, "Why don't we ask the students what they think?" By conducting their study of DSP through the frame of user experience (UX) design, the authors are able to investigate their campus tools through the eyes of students, rather than solely from within the administrative mindset. Their usability study of DSP for online FYW courses demonstrates both how localized assessment methods are vital to develop equitable practices and ways that WPAs can go about doing research through those methods.

As many of our institutions face budget cuts, pressures to raise enrollment caps rise. In "Building Effective Arguments about Writing Class Size and Workload," Todd Ruecker and Galen Gorlangton share results from an interview-based study of arguments that twenty WPAs from various institutional contexts have used to resist increases in class size. The interviews reveal that a humanities background often creates challenges for WPAs who are called to advocate for their programs within the corporate and efficiency-driven frameworks that now dominate higher education. Based on their interviews with WPAs at Hispanic-Serving Institutions (HSIs), two-year colleges (TYCs), and Historically Black Colleges and Universities (HBCUs), Ruecker and Gorelangton also highlight the patterns of disparity in how effective certain arguments are in different contexts, most notably along lines of race and class. The article, however, isn't just about the challenges WPAs encounter: Ruecker and Gorelangton share several rhetorical strategies WPAs use to resist the discourses of cost-effectiveness when pressed to increase class sizes. We hope readers will come away from the piece with ideas for how they, like the WPAs mentioned in the article, might connect the work of their programs to administrative priorities and create strategic alliances with other units on campus and in the communities surrounding their institutions.

Teresa Thonney examines first-year composition courses from 164 community and technical colleges across the US to determine if what is taught in them really prepares students for writing in other disciplines. In "Are We Preparing Students to Write across the Curriculum?: An Analysis of Learning Outcomes for First-Year Composition at Two-Year Colleges," Thonney categorizes the skills or focuses in first-year composition courses evident in the courses she surveyed. She then shares her findings from collecting samples of student writing from faculty at her institution. Thonney discusses that while the first-year composition courses focus on the skills that would help students write across disciplines, the writing students do in these disciplines often does not demonstrate transfer of the first-year composition skills. Thonney argues for professional development and discussions among two-year college faculty on transfer that may result in revised learning objectives in the first-year composition courses at these schools to explicitly focus on transfer.

Reviews

The issue concludes with two book reviews. First, Hunter Little offers prospective readers an administrative lens through which to approach *Writing Knowledge Transfer: Theory, Research, and Pedagogy* by Rebecca S. Nowacek, Rebecca Lorimer Leonard, and Angela Rounsaville. She introduces the book as an extensive study on the role of knowledge transfer within and beyond the field of writing studies, and she offers WPAs possible connections between Nowacek, Lorimer Leonard, and Rounsaville's research and curriculum development as well as professional development in college writing programs. Little also emphasizes the authors' work in associating knowledge transfer and embodied cognition, which she suggests might be of particular interest to readers interested in the intersections of writing program administration and disability scholarship. Little encourages readers to approach *Writing Knowledge Transfer* with a transdisciplinary mindset and openness toward unifying transfer perspectives across disciplines.

Finally, in his review of Darin Jensen and Brett Griffiths's *Two-Year College Writing Studies: Rationale and Praxis for Just Teaching*, Donny Penner shares the joy of reading a text centered on and for two-year college faculty. He acknowledges the lack of conversation about two-year colleges in the field, and particularly its graduate curricula; and he recommends anyone interested in teaching writing take up Jensen and Griffiths's collection as an introduction to administrative and activist efforts in community colleges. He encourages readers to approach *Two-Year College Writing Studies* as a starting point for addressing longstanding issues regarding labor, professionalization, and linguistic justice in this context.

Conclusion

As you can see from our overview of this issue, editing *WPA: Writing Program Administration* provides the opportunity to participate in and shape rich disciplinary discussions. Part of our goal as an editorial team has been to include perspectives that represent the broad range of WPA experiences, and we hope we've achieved that. As you read the current issue, we invite you to think about how you might like to expand the conversations and consider applying to be part of the next editorial team.

Everything Is Praxis

Overenrolled for the Summer: Graduate Instructor Labor, Course Caps, and Other Compounding Impacts

Gavin P. Johnson, Yu Lei, Rachel McShane, Haomei Meng, Reza Panahi, and Gouda Taha

Abstract

In this brief article, we—a group of graduate students and a WPA—reflect on the challenges faced during a recent summer session. In doing so, we consider how our experience speaks to a larger issue: the compounding impacts that dictate the pedagogical and administrative decisions that need to be made within a writing program. Compounding impacts, as a concept, describes how local classroom concerns and programmatic logistics accumulate and exacerbate labor disparities and pedagogical challenges. Specifically, we consider the various changes necessitated when graduate students acting as instructors of record are assigned to teach overenrolled first-year writing courses during a compressed, five-week summer session. From our experience, we outline compounding impacts on labor related to course planning, class activities and management, and assessment as well as issues of financial precarity and international student status. We conclude with the list of suggestions we provided our local administration in the hopes that readers can understand how we blended scholarship and experience into praxis as well as anticipate similar impacts at their colleges and universities.

Introduction and Context

Graduate teaching assistants work hard. They exist in a liminal space of both student and teacher while acting as instructors of record while simultaneously taking seminars, preparing for comprehensive exams, designing and conducting research, attending professional development sessions, and, not to mention, living lives beyond the campus that often include family commitments, caregiving responsibilities, financial precarity, friendships, and long-distance relationships. It is quite a lot to juggle in ideal circumstances (for example, when life is going smoothly, courses are engaging, and we are teaching smaller classes during a full 15-week semester with little to no calendar shifts); when other complications arise, such as larger classes, shortened semesters, or financial or personal struggles, things become challenging to balance, and that labor becomes less tenable.

The labor demanded by first-year writing programs has increasingly been documented and studied. Spurred on by the historic work of the Wyoming Resolution (see Robertson, Crowley, & Lentricchia, 1987) and later the Indianapolis Resolution (see Cox et al., 2016), scholars including Seth Kahn (2015), Nancy Welch and Tony Scott (2016), and Randall McClure, Dayna V. Goldstein, and Michael A. Pemberton (2017) have passionately argued that the labor of teaching composition, especially under neoliberal austerity measures, cannot be ignored when it makes lives within the academy so precarious. Often the most exploitative labor is hoisted upon non-tenure track faculty, contingent instructors, and graduate students; however, the experiences of these communities are rarely considered when administrative decisions are made. We aim to use this space to take seriously Ruth Osorio, Jaclyn Fiscus-Cannaday, and Allison Hutchinson's (2021) call to collect stories, honor lived experiences, and move toward collaborative leadership models with and for graduate students who teach writing.

We are colleagues—five graduate teaching assistants and one faculty member—working and learning in a PhD program housed in a department that offers courses and research opportunities in a range of disciplines and specializations: literary studies, rhetoric and writing studies, and applied linguistics. While not all PhD students apply for a teaching position in the first-year writing program, those who teach typically maintain their appointment throughout their degree program, pending acceptable progress toward degree and annual evaluation of teaching. In our program, students with Graduate Assistant Teaching (GAT[1]) appointments teach a majority of first-year writing classes—anywhere from 60–88% of sections offered. They typically teach two sections of first-year writing as instructors of record during fall and spring semesters. Summer is split into two five-week mini-sessions, and GATs have an opportunity to teach one course in each session. However, summer teaching is never guaranteed. GATs can express their interest, but ultimately, enrollment dictates availability. Regardless of how many summer courses are offered, it is not unusual for GATs to teach all but one or two of the summer offerings of first-year writing.

The writing program houses three first-year writing courses: English 1302: Written Research/Argument, English 1301: College Reading and Writing, and English 100: Introduction to College Reading and Writing (a corequisite basic writing course linked to English 1301). English 1301 and English 1302 are the only courses on campus that currently satisfy the "Written and Oral Communication" requirement of the Texas Core

Curriculum (TCC). In line with professional standards, class enrollment caps are set at eighteen students for English 1301 and 1302 and twelve students for English 100 (CCCC, 2023). The writing program provides a born-digital custom textbook and skeletal outline of the curriculum, but GATs are responsible for drafting course schedules, developing daily lesson plans, delivering instruction, assessing and responding to student assignments, and general classroom management. All things considered, the writing program is typical for a university like ours––a rural, teaching-focused, emerging R2 institution with a diverse student population in terms of age, race, and socioeconomic status.

While the return to face-to-face instruction following Covid-induced virtual learning has led many universities to struggle with recruitment, Texas A&M University-Commerce[1] experienced a surge in enrollment (Segar, 2023a). This increase is related to shifts expanding admission policies, adjusting student placement protocols, and general administrative decision-making related to the university mission. The university president, according to an announcement to the campus, believes the surge in enrollment is a "testament to the institution's unwavering commitment to providing quality education and a supportive community for all students . . . providing a gateway to success for its growing student body" (Segar, 2023a). We are proud to be a part of this growing campus community, which continues to be named one of the best schools for social mobility in the United States (Segar, 2023b). We, in turn, work diligently to ensure that our curriculum and pedagogy align with the needs of the students that come to our classes. However, we also recognize, through this brief article, that this kind of rapid, newsworthy growth has a direct impact on the labor of first-year writing courses and the instructors, specifically GATs, at the front of the classroom.

We began to feel the impact of the student enrollment surge in the second summer session of 2023 (Summer II 2023). This session was five weeks of intensive instruction, four days a week, and was understandably already difficult for instructors because of the speed and labor required to ensure students receive "equivalent experiences" to their peers in a 15-week regular semester, as the university expects. With high demand and low supply, the required nature of the courses, and independent choices made by upper administration and advisors––despite the director of writing and

---

1. As of November 7, 2024, our university has been renamed East Texas A&M University. Because this article was in final proofing at the time of this change, we have decided to maintain the university name used during the events described within.

department head pushing to maintain the standard enrollment caps—our courses quickly overenrolled. Most instructors, with little notice, taught courses with at least three to seven students above the enrollment cap. While overenrollment by one or two students in one or two sections is not uncommon at our university, to have nearly every course overenrolled by such a large number was a concern that presented issues for students, GATs, and the director of writing.

A Note on Our Composing Process

Consider this a conversation. On October 11, 2023, Gavin P. Johnson, in his role as director of writing, met with five GATs—coauthors. Yu Lei, Rachel McShane, Haomei Meng, Reza Panahi, and Gouda Taha. This meeting took place over Zoom, and we discussed the GATs' experience teaching basic and first-year writing during Summer II 2023 (July 10–August 10, 2023). Our conversation was structured around eleven questions that Johnson prepared prior to the meeting (see appendix). By request of the department head, and with a small stipend, our primary task was crafting a memo for upper administration documenting and making recommendations for future scheduling, staffing, and GAT support.

During the conversation, Johnson considered how valuable this discussion might be not only for our institution but also for WPAs and graduate students in similar situations. He proposed that the group co-write a short article culled from the conversation. Using the Zoom recordings and automated transcripts, Johnson crafted the internal memo and shared it with the GATs to ensure they were accurately represented. To craft this article, we expanded our original memo to include additional context and scholarly framing to our conversation. Johnson composed the first draft before circulating it for Lei, McShane, Meng, Panahi, and Taha to offer feedback, make additions, and redirect the argument as needed. After receiving enthusiastic and valuable feedback from two *WPA: Writing Program Administration* reviewers, McShane and her fellow GATs took the lead revising for resubmission before sharing their draft with Johnson.

Our goal with this article is to demonstrate the impact of compounding factors, including course overenrollment, on the labor demanded from GATs teaching writing. Compounding impacts, as we use it, describes how local classroom concerns and programmatic logistics accumulate and exacerbate labor disparities and pedagogical challenges. This concept captures the entanglement of issues that feed into large-scale problems and, in turn, grow labor disparities. Put simply: it's never just one thing; or, when it rains it pours. Below we briefly discuss select literature available on the impact of class size on pedagogical and programmatic decisions. Then, we make note of our major points of discussion, which we believe directly influenced our teaching and administrative experiences. Finally, we offer thoughts on how to address the challenges of overenrolled writing-intensive courses, speaking not only to the graduate students teaching these courses but also writing program administrators and other decision makers.

The Issue of Class Size

Conversations about appropriate class size are certainly not new. In our research, we were amazed to find monographs and articles from the early 20th century debating the impact of the student-to-teacher ratio (Stevenson, 1923; Hatfield, 1924). Then, as now, much of the debate concerns tensions between the quality of learning and administrative efficiency. Alice Horning (2007) went as far as to say, "if you are a WPA, sooner or later, you are going to have a fight with your administration over class size" (p. 11). Horning, like others, argued that smaller class sizes are preferable as their benefits impact student success, faculty labor, and institutional reputation. These arguments have continued to grow in importance as austerity measures taken by universities often begin with enlarging class enrollment caps (Cuseo, 2007; Phillips & Ahrenhoerster, 2018). And while we acknowledge recent pedagogical experimentation with "jumbo" and "MonsterComp" writing courses (Jaxon, Sparks, & Fosen, 2020; Seigel et al., 2020), for our institutional context, the writing program curriculum was designed for small(er) class sizes.

According to the Conference on College Composition and Communication (2023),

- **No more than 20 students should be permitted in any writing class. Ideally, classes should be limited to 15.**
- **No English faculty members should teach more than 60 writing students per term. Any more than this, and teachers are spread too thin to effectively engage with students on their writing.**
(The Enabling Conditions section, no. 11, para. 2)

These enrollment caps are noticeably lower than other first-year courses because of the immense labor that teaching writing involves, including extensive engagement with student writing processes and assignment drafts. Our first-year writing courses currently include enrollment caps that are in line with these recommendations: English 100 has a cap of 12; English 1301/1302 have caps of 18; GATs and adjuncts teach no more than two courses per term while lecturers teach five courses per term. These recommendations were developed to provide "reasonable and equitable working conditions" to writing instructors ("A&M-Commerce," 2019). Our enrollment caps were established after an active push from a previous director of writing and a previous department head only a few years prior. In fact, the then-recent reduction in course caps was explicitly mentioned as a contributing factor in the writing program receiving a CCCC Writing Program Certificate of Excellence ("A&M-Commerce," 2019).

These reasonable course caps are still our starting point; however, exceeding those caps has become a frequent issue. Surging enrollments and restricted staffing budgets mean a course capped at 18 often has an actual enrollment of 20+. Students are frequently added over the cap by their advisors and with the consent of the department head. We do not see these actions as malicious as, often, they are trying to help a student. The issue comes when one student is added above the cap . . . then another . . . then another . . . compounding the impact. While we continue pushing for respecting the enrollment caps, it seemingly is a never-ending defensive position wherein we must carefully negotiate disciplinary best practices, instructor labor, student learning, and the influence of our university's shifting demographics and administrative expectations. This was the issue during Summer II 2023 when most first-year writing courses were overenrolled.

Impacts of Overenrollment

In what follows, we synthesize our conversations within the context and scholarship discussed above. Namely, we make note of three impact factors experienced during Summer II 2023: impact on course planning, impact on class activities and course management, and impact on assessment. These are offered so that readers gain more insight about our experiences but also, if put into similar positions, they can feel prepared.

Impact on Course Planning

In our conversations, all five GATs reported no change to their initial course planning due to overenrollment, per se, since enrollments were not finalized before the start of the term. What did drastically impact course planning was the compressed summer session as they reported difficulty fitting the program's curriculum into a 5-week summer course. For Lei and Meng, while they had experience teaching the curriculum previously, this was their first time teaching a summer course. Lei explained, "I feel it's pretty intensive. I taught from Monday to Thursday about two hours a day." Meng added,

It's very stressful because I also have two summer courses. You know the courses I registered for myself. So from Monday to Thursday, I feel that I'm overburdened. And the other feeling is that, you know, in the spring and the fall semesters, I can ask students to do more things than in summer because time is quite limited. So I feel that there are some things that I haven't conveyed to my students.

Having to balance courses while learning how to deliver the content and support students was challenging. Certainly, while teaching under new constraints always tests our pedagogical choices, the intensity of a summer course doesn't leave space to make the kind of *in situ* adjustments an instructor might make during a 15-week semester. Many of those decisions about what to keep or cut should be made prior to starting the summer term.

McShane and Panahi have taught summer courses before and knew what they were in for. When asked about the labor of planning, McShane explained, "If I'm completely honest because I taught [English 1301] so many times, it didn't impact my course planning that much . . . I could recycle PowerPoints and things like that." Panahi echoed this approach. These GATs later noted that without previous experience teaching during the summer, they likely could not have managed planning and delivering the course, particularly in an overenrollment situation with more students to work with.

Impact on Class Activities and Management

While they did not feel too challenged by planning their course, the GATs did report a noticeable impact on their approach to class activities and class management. Due to the combination of the overenrollment and a condensed term, Meng reported relying less on lecturing and made use of additional small group work and collective discussions to get through the material and maintain opportunities for in-class writing support. Lei also embraced more in-class workshopping to help students set aside time to write. We recognize that these shifts can be read as beneficial since they allowed for more process-oriented and collaborative class time. That is a silver lining; however, Lei found it difficult to work directly with students in her English 100 course. She expressed concern that students were always waiting for her to make it around the classroom. During our conversation, the GATs took this time to discuss their own methods of assigning informal reading partners and peer reviewers to ensure everyone was getting some kind of one-on-one attention, which alleviates some pressure for the instructor, but does not, in their opinion, have the same impact as instructor guidance.

Interestingly, while attendance proved to be a consistent problem during regular semesters, especially after the return to face-to-face instruction following Covid-19 lockdowns, the GATs felt that attendance during the summer was stronger than the recent spring and fall semesters with more students attending more often and participating more. We don't quite know why this happened. Perhaps students recognized that missing a class session on a compressed timeline would prove much more detrimental to their learning.[2] Taha noted that his attendance was not only steady but that students were also reaching out to him via email much more frequently. This level of engagement, according to Taha, led to some surprisingly strong writing. While this is a hopeful and typically exciting occurrence for teachers, especially after a period of low attendance and engagement, overenrollment created tension, making it difficult for the GATs to appreciate this positive change. Stronger attendance and engagement of students in this situation meant more effort was required from instructors on group activities, class management, and communication with students, and they found it somewhat overwhelming to try and meet the demands of large and active classes within the constraints.

Class management was difficult for some GATs, especially those who had several students with advising mix-ups as well as exceedingly high enrollments. McShane reflected,

> When I first started teaching summer, and this was some years ago, the cap for summer and fall was not the same. The cap, I believe, for summer was 15 while fall and spring semesters were capped at 18; now summer classes are capped at 18 just like the regular 15-week semester. I started this class with 26 students on the first day because of a mix- up in advising. So these students that should have been in another class were all in my class for like two weeks. The classroom management was tough, like the hardest I've ever had. I usually can harness a chatty class and keep on task, but this was just talking, talking, talking. Every single seat in my classroom was full. Every single seat. And most of them had another class right before mine. They were just antsy to the max. And it was exhausting.

Again, this demonstrates the way two issues overlapped: the overenrollment caused a literal crowding in the room, while the intense summer schedule caused students and instructors to feel particularly burnt out and to act accordingly. This created tension in the classroom for both the teacher and the students. In addition, we can see the pressure that inaccurate placement brought, highlighting the need to continue refining procedures to ensure students are appropriately placed. Despite years of teaching experience, McShane often found teaching difficult in this situation, regardless of the classroom strategies she tried.

Impact on Assessment

By far, courses being enrolled above standard caps had the largest and most negative impact on the assessment of student writing. During the conversation all GATs continued returning to the point of assessment because it had such a dominant impact on their time, energy, and labor. Taha, who has a scholarly interest in assessment, noted:

> More students means you need to spend much more time on grading and giving feedback, especially providing the kind of detailed feedback students need for revision. In this case you're trying to provide some constructive feedback, not just praising feedback––good job or excellent––but I didn't have the time.

This sentiment was repeated over, and over, and over again.

Due to the number of students and the speed of the semester, general advice might be for an instructor to reduce the amount and specificity of feedback they are giving on drafts. However, McShane felt that approach was a "disservice to the students." She estimated spending "probably twice as much time [assessing papers and] the turnover rate is much faster. In the spring or fall, I could take two weeks to grade papers, and now I have to get it done in like two days."

Even if a GAT was comfortable reducing the amount of feedback provided, the labor was still intense when added to tasks like planning lectures, attending seminars, reading for exams, or conducting research. Panahi explained, "Imagine the professor is also working on his proposal, or he has some assignment to do and, also, teaching. It is a lot of work, and you get stressed." Panahi, pressured by the number of documents to respond to and his other commitments, did experiment with more holistic forms of feedback and more explicit student peer-to-peer assessments and support structures. He found this very impactful and planned to bring it into his future courses too.

While not a focus of the prepared questions, some GATs believe several students used text generating AI like ChatGPT to complete coursework. McShane noted that she discovered a student misused ChatGPT throughout the term and had to not only fail the student but was also required to report the student for plagiarism, which created additional labor. Meng made a point to include a short discussion about ChatGPT in her class, but still suspected unauthorized use by students rushing to produce writing. This practice led to "difficult conversations with students." Panahi agreed and noted that he felt that the conversation was important to have but felt unsure how to address the issue, especially when time was so limited. In a typical 15-week semester with a regular-sized class, teachers might have had the opportunity to explore ChatGPT as a tool, invite a librarian to facilitate a workshop on ethical AI use, and encourage students to critically engage with generative AI programs; however, in a class that was overenrolled and crammed into five weeks, it simply created more labor and frustration for GATs, especially when attempting to provide feedback on a towering stack of student writing.

Other Compounding Impacts

As it goes, the challenges that face professionals in higher education are never singular but rather compounding. As we have explained, our point of discussion, teaching and coordinating Summer II 2023 first-year writing courses at Texas A&M University-Commerce, concerns not only the issue of overenrolled courses but also overenrolled courses that were on a time-compressed (5-week) schedule.

Summer courses, for many, offer an opportunity for students to either "catch up" or "get ahead" in their coursework, especially general education courses. While studies of time-compressed instruction show insignificant declines in student performance and, in fact, can positively impact certain subjects, "reading- and writing-intensive courses" that are time-compressed show mostly negative impacts on student learning (Martin & Culver, 2005; Lutes & Davies, 2018). This is not surprising, we're sure, to those aligned with process pedagogy, collaborative writing, and iterative revision. Compressed terms simply don't offer temporal space for those activities, and overenrolled courses further limit time and space for learning.

Writing teachers also feel the time-compression, as noted again and again in our earlier discussion. Instructors commonly make major adjustments in pedagogical approach, assignment lengths, and student assessment instruments to keep pace with the course. Mark A. Kretovics, Alicia R. Crowe, and Eunsook Hyun (2005) studied faculty perceptions of summer courses on their teaching and found that while most instructors adjusted their curricula to accommodate for the summer, faculty status and rank significantly influenced the instructor's willingness to deviate from a full-term teaching approach. Specifically, tenured and tenure-track faculty studied were more willing to adjust courses than nontenured instructors, which Kretovis, Crow, and Hyun (2005) attribute to concerns about labor and "political stability" (pp. 46–48). This point is essential to understanding the pressures felt by GATs teaching summer courses.

Extrapolating from these findings, we must consider the pressure placed on GATs who experience significant precarity and shifting identities: "caught in [a] special type of bureaucratic and professional purgatory; at once a teacher *and* student" (Marine, 2023). In our department, GATs are not guaranteed summer funding, and because of their student status, if they do take on a summer teaching assignment they must be enrolled in coursework or independent dissertation research hours: three out of five GATs were taking one or more summer courses and two were registered for dissertation research hours.

In addition to the aforementioned impacts, all GATs cited financial instability as a reason for taking on summer teaching. Indeed, while they all would have liked to use their summer to focus on their coursework or research, they needed to teach to have an income, albeit an income roughly half their fall/spring pay since most GATs could only be assigned one course. McShane said that without a summer appointment, she would have had to seek out other temporary employment. However, for the other four international GATs, that is not an option; international students visas prohibit working beyond the context of education unless the student applies for Curricular Practical Training (CPT), which also has restrictions. As explained in the nextGEN (2020) Advocacy Call to Challenge Institutionalized Xenophobia Against International Students, "International students face significant financial burdens for not being allowed to work off campus during the semester. Moreover, as nonimmigrant residents, they often do not qualify for many financial aid and scholarship opportunities that would help defray the cost." That is, Lei, Meng, Panahi, and Taha virtually had no way of making money over the summer—to pay rent, buy groceries, seek medical care, support a family, or travel home for the summer—without taking on coursework and a teaching appointment for a 5-week, overenrolled writing course. Graduate students can also be appointed to research assistantships; however, those appointments are virtually non-existent meaning for many a teaching appointment is essential.

Like the GATs, the director of writing does not have guaranteed summer funding because of a 9-month faculty contract. For summer 2023, Johnson did receive a teaching appointment during Summer I 2023 as well as an administrative appointment for Summer II 2023. His administrative appointment, while related to the writing program, was provided for him to complete the year-long revision of the program's born-digital textbook. He diverted some of his time to supporting the summer courses; however, without that additional appointment, any support he would have provided would have been unpaid labor.

While compressed summer terms, instructor status, and financial strains are not inherently linked to the issue of overenrollment, they should be critically considered in this conversation as they compound on each other significantly increasing the impact felt. GATs needed to accept the appointments, regardless of the increased labor and stress, because of limited opportunities for summer funding and/or restrictive employment rules. This results in GATs feeling physically and mentally fatigued trying to keep up with the demands of an overenrolled class and emotionally exhausted due to worry and concern of finances, which also leads to an inability to fully engage with all the students. Meanwhile, the director of writing is often required to choose between supporting GATs via unpaid labor or simply leaving them unsupported. Meng perhaps described our collective affect during Summer II 2023 best: "overburdened."

Suggestions to Administrators

As detailed above, Summer II 2023 was challenging on multiple fronts. Most obviously, overenrollment increased the labor and stress on not only GATs but also students and the director of writing. When asked to create a memo for upper administration detailing the various challenges, we (Johnson, Lei, McShane, Meng, Panahi, and Taha) provided the suggestions below. We are also providing these here for readers to consider and, potentially, advocate for at their own institutions.

- **Actively abide by the course enrollment caps and consider the potential of even lower caps for summer courses** that are more intensive because of the condensed 5-week term. Strict adherence to the enrollment caps needs to be communicated to other university offices with the ability to enroll students.
- **Continue refining placement procedures so that students who opt to enroll in summer courses are placed appropriately.** This work is currently underway thanks to a grant from the Texas Higher Education Coordinating Board (THECB); however, that grant specifically focuses on English 100. We should also consider placement procedures in English 1301 and 1302, which could provide not only more accurate placement but allow for more accurate scheduling from the department. This is assuming that more accurate placement procedures would shift enrollments.
- **Offer additional professional development opportunities that provide GATs strategies for addressing logistical issues**, like over-

enrollment, while reducing negative impact on otherwise professionally sound pedagogical approaches.
- **Continue working to address issues with GAT salaries and summer funding opportunities.** Our funding structure does not necessarily allow GATs to prepare for summer financial obligations during the regular term. Further, by linking teaching appointments with required courses, we are not only requiring heavy workloads balancing teaching and coursework/dissertation research but also requiring students to pay fees that further reduce their already limited summer income. Overenrolling the courses they teach, moreover, asks GATs to do additional labor without additional compensation.[3]
    - In particular, international GATs are in a precarious position as their ability to find alternative employment during the summer is restricted. This requires them to accept (indeed, actively request) these summer appointments, regardless of workload or impact on their own coursework, research, or personal wellness.
- **Consider the possibility of teaching full summer term (10 week) sections of the writing classes.**
- **Work to notify GATs of summer appointments earlier.** Current practice means GATs are rarely made aware of their appointments more than two weeks in advance of the start of term. Additional time to prepare would be beneficial.
- **Continue the practice of providing a course equivalent of reassigned time for the director of writing during the summer terms.** While the director of writing was granted reassigned time during Summer II 2023, this is not guaranteed as a 9-month employee. Considering the amount of support needed during the summer terms, the director must be compensated. This time can also be used to prepare for the upcoming semesters and attend to important tasks such as programmatic assessment or curricular development.

The lessons we learned during a hectic summer term are localized praxis. We engaged in our group conversations and composed this article to theorize—make sense of—our experiences within the larger context of labor in first-year writing. As we continue working to address issues of labor, student success, and administrative support for writing programs, it is essential to remember and attend to the compounding impacts affecting the experience of graduate students who teach.

Coda

We are revising this article during the Summer II and Fall 2024 terms. Reflecting on the issue of summer overenrollment and the compounding labor issues experienced during Summer II 2023, we find ourselves in an unenviable situation. While none of the courses taught by GATs were overenrolled in Summer I or II, that is by chance and due to faculty members allowing their courses to be overenrolled. Generally, labor conditions have not improved significantly, regardless of our feedback to upper administration. And, unfortunately, the enrollments for the Fall 2024 semester far exceeded our staffing capacity and quickly swelled beyond our strongly fought for course caps. Currently, we are seeing that many of the issues experienced during our overenrolled summer courses are emerging during the 15-week session. These actions have not simply happened but are part and parcel for ongoing budgetary shifts and hiring restrictions within higher education and our university as well as a weak culture of communication between units on campus.

Being here, again, does not mean we haven't been working to make good on our recommendations. Johnson carefully advocated for setting the GAT summer teaching appointments earlier, and he was able to notify instructors about their appointments earlier than normal. This advanced notice provided instructors opportunities to better plan their summer labor and expenses. Additionally, new methods for student placement and realigned curricula are making the co-requisite English 100 and English 1301 course more efficient providing the intensive writing support commonly needed among the still-surging student populations. On the issue of finances, while not in place for Summer 2024, thanks to the dedicated work of our PhD coordinator, GATs now (retitled Graduate Assistant Instructors of Record, or GAToRs) receive their regular stipend and tuition waiver as well as have their fees covered keeping more money in their pockets: upwards of $1,600 per semester. In terms of professional development, workshops focusing on balancing the competing identities that GATs inhabit as student and teacher were offered during the pre-semester writing program orientation and plans are developing to offer sessions on assessment and encouraging student attendance and participation. Next, with McShane recently being hired as one of two full-time lecturers, Johnson established The Writing Program Council to collaboratively push for improved labor conditions. Finally, with the encouragement our interim department head, Johnson is implementing new guardrails for assigning and enrolling courses, and a request for additional full-time lecturers has been submitted. Stabilizing our teaching faculty, we hope, will relieve some of the enrollment pressure and, eventually, allow for graduate students teach advanced undergraduate courses in their area of study.

In short, we are doing what we can at the local level to move our goals forward and counter the impacts that are continually compounding.

Acknowledgments

We would like to thank Ashanka Kumari for giving feedback on an early draft of this article and for tirelessly fighting for graduate student empowerment and equity in our department. Additionally, we thank Ruth Osorio and a second anonymous peer reviewer for their thorough and kind recommendations. Authorship on this article is happily shared equally among the authors—everyone put in 100%.

Notes

1. Our PhD coordinator, and former director of writing, has worked diligently with the dean of the graduate school to implement a title that indicates the enhanced labor taken on by graduate students independently teaching sections of first-year writing. As of fall 2024, their title is "Graduate Assistant Teacher of Record" (GAToR).

2. This theory is supported by the fact that many of the Summer II students are part of a bridge program wherein they are provisionally accepted to the university but must pass their summer courses with a grade of C or higher.

3. In summer 2023 the department head and director of writing were able to pay each of the GATs with overenrolled classes a small supplement to their stipend. Although the stipend was minimal, it made a difference to the GATs who have often taught extra students but never received compensation. McShane commented, "I've taught overenrolled courses almost every semester for the last four years and have never received any extra pay for all the additional labor, so even though the stipend was small, it was nice to finally feel recognized and acknowledged for all my work."

References

"A&M-Commerce writing program receives certificate of excellence." (2019, January. 18). *Texas A&M University-Commerce News*. https://www.tamuc.edu/news/am-commerce-writing-program-receives-certificate-of-excellence/

CCCC statement on principles for the postsecondary teaching of writing. (2023). NCTE/CCCC. https://cccc.ncte.org/cccc/resources/positions/postsecondarywriting

Cox, Anicca, Dougherty, Timothy R., Kahn, Seth, LaFrance, Michelle, & Lynch-Biniek, Amy. (2016). The Indianapolis Resolution: Responding to twenty-first-century exigencies/political economies of composition labor. *College Composition and Communication, 68*(1), 38–67.

Cuseo, Joe. (2007). The empirical case against large class size: Adverse effects on the teach, learning, and retention of first-year students. *The Journal of Faculty Development, 1,* 5–21.

Hatfield, W. Wilbur. (1924). Review: Smaller classes or larger? *The English Journal, 13*(2), 152–153.

Horning, Alice. (2007). The definitive article on class size. *WPA: Writing Program Administration, 31*(1–2), 11–34.

Jaxon, Kim, Sparks, Laura, & Fosen, Chris. (2020). Epic learning in a "jumbo" writing course. *Composition Studies, 48*(2), 116–127.

Kahn, Seth. (2015). Towards an ecology of sustainable labor in writing programs (and other places). *WPA: Writing Program Administration, 39*(1), 109–122.

Kretovics, Mark A., Crowe, Alicia R., & Hyun, Eunsook. (2005). A study of faculty perceptions of summer compressed course teaching. *Innovative Higher Education, 30*(1), 37–51.

Lutes, Lyndell, & Davies, Randall. (2018). Comparison of workload for university core courses taught in regular semester and time-compressed term formats. *Education Sciences, 8*(1), 1–12. https://doi.org/10.3390/educsci8010034

Marine, Jonathan M. (2023). Narrative 5. Student, teacher, teaching assistant: Janus and institutional identity. In William J. Macauley, Jr., Leslie R. Anglesey, Brady Edwards, Kathryn M. Lambrecht, & Phillip K. Lovas (Eds.), *Threshold Conscripts: Rhetoric and Composition Teaching Assistantships* (pp. 165–166). The WAC Clearinghouse; University Press of Colorado.

Martin, Howard, & Culver, Kathleen Bartzen. (2005). To concentrate, to intensify, or to shorten? The issue of the short intensive course in summer sessions. *Summer Academe, 6,* 59–69.

McClure, Randall, Goldstein, Dayna V., & Pemberton, Michael A. (Eds). (2017). *Labored: The state(ment) and future of work in composition.* Parlor Press.

nextGen. (2020). Advocacy call to challenge institutionalized xenophobia against international students. Retrieved from https://docs.google.com/document/d/1GCkZpfGz6c3h6L9xMj1ppzgdm26shD8E-TaoyTnITLw/edit?usp=sharing

Osorio, Ruth, Fiscus-Cannaday, Jaclyn, & Hutchinson, Allison (2021). Braiding stories, taking action: A narrative of graduate worker-led change work. In Holly Hassel & Kristi Cole (Eds.) *Transformations: Change work across writing programs, pedagogies, and practices.* University Press of Colorado.

Phillips, Cassandra & Ahrenhoerster, Greg (2018). Class size and first-year writing: Exploring the effects on pedagogy and student perception of writing process. *Teaching English in the Two Year College, 46*(1), 9–29. https://doi.org/10.58680/tetyc201829823

Robertson, Linda R., Crowley, Sharon, & Lentricchia, Frank. (1987). The Wyoming Conference Resolution opposing unfair salaries and working conditions for post-secondary teachers of writing. *College English, 49,* 274–80. https://doi.org/10.2307/377922

Segar, Kristen. (2023a, November 9). A&M-Commerce emerges as the fastest-growing public university in Texas. *Texas A&M University-Commerce News.* https://www.tamuc.edu/news/am-commerce-emerges-as-the-fastest-growing-public-university-in-texas/

Segar, Kristen. (2023b, November 1). U.S. News & World Report ranks A&M-Commerce #58 in the nation for social mobility. *Texas A&M University-Commerce News.* https://www.tamuc.edu/u-s-news-world-report-ranks-am-commerce-58-in-the-nation-for-social-mobility/

Seigel, Marika, Chase, Josh, De Herder, William, Feltz, Silke, Kitalong, Karla Saari, Romney, Abraham, & Tweedale, Kimerly. (2020). Monstrous composition: Reanimating the lecture in first-year writing instruction. *College Composition and Communication, 71*(4), 643–671. https://doi.org/10.58680/ccc202030728

Stevenson, Paul Raymond. (1923). *Smaller classes or larger. A study of the relation of class-size to the efficiency of teaching.* Public School Publishing Company.

Welch, Nancy, & Scott, Tony. (Eds.). (2016). *Composition in the age of austerity.* University Press of Colorado.

Appendix: Questions for October 11th Meeting with GATs

1. What was the general feeling teaching during Summer II?
2. Did the overenrollment of students impact or increase time spent course planning? How or by about how much time?
3. Did the overenrollment of students impact how you ran your class? How?
4. Did the overenrollment of students impact or increase time spent assessing student writing? How or by about how much time?
5. Based on final course grades, was student success potentially impacted by the overenrollment?
6. Beyond Summer II 2023, have you taught overenrolled classes at TAMUC?
    a. If so, how often?
    b. If so, how did it impact your teaching or student success?
7. Did receiving a summer appointment impact your financial stability?
8. Did the one-time additional payment impact your financial stability?
9. If you would not have received a summer appointment, would you have sought other employment?
10. Would you have focused on your research?
11. Any final comments?

Gavin P. Johnson, PhD (he/him) currently works as director of writing and assistant professor at East Texas A&M University (formerly Texas A&M University-Commerce). His research interests include critical digital pedagogy, multimodal composition, antioppressive writing assessment, queer-feminist rhetorics, and surveillance studies. He has won numerous national awards including the 2024 Ellen Nold Award for Outstanding Article in Computers and Composition Studies with Laura L. Allen. Gavin is a proud first-generation college graduate from southeast Louisiana.

Yu Lei, PhD (she/her) is a doctoral student studying applied linguistics. Her current research interests focus on humor and computer-mediated communications. She teaches courses in basic and first-year writing and has previously taught courses in Chinese language. She received her first PhD from Beijing Language and Culture University in China.

Rachel McShane, PhD (she/her) currently works as a lecturer in the writing program at East Texas A&M University (formerly Texas A&M University-Commerce). Her dissertation research focused on rhetorical framings of womanhood and studied three cases of Texas women who stood trial for murder and were found guilty. Rachel teaches courses in basic, first-year, and advanced writing. As a graduate student, Rachel won one of four inaugural Innovations in Writing Pedagogy Awards from the writing program.

Haomei Meng (she/her) is studies applied linguistics, cognition, and humor. She teaches courses in basic and first-year writing.

Reza Panahi, PhD (he/him) is a doctoral candidate studying applied linguistics and online language education. He teaches courses in basic and first-year writing and won one of four inaugural Innovations in Writing Pedagogy Awards in 2024 from the writing program.

Gouda Taha (he/him) is a doctoral candidate studying applied linguistics, second-language pedagogy, assessment, and AI in the classroom. He teaches courses in basic and first-year writing and won one of four inaugural Innovations in Writing Pedagogy Awards in 2024 from the writing program.

FAQ: Developing & Maintaining Shared Curriculum

Mariya Tseptsura and Rochelle Rodrigo

Abstract

Although writing programs have a long history of using both required and optional shared curricular materials (e.g., syllabus templates, major assignment prompts, textbooks), the current use of completely developed, pre-designed courses has triggered many scholarly discussions about the reasons for and against using shared curricular materials. This FAQ provides a detailed outline of ways to define and conceptualize shared curriculum as well as considerations for developing, sharing, maintaining, and administering shared curricular materials. The answers in the FAQ include discussions of instructor authority and professionalism, stakeholder influence, and administrative logistics and policies.

It is not an overstatement to say that most writing programs have long been relying on shared curriculum in some way, from using syllabus templates to adopting common textbooks or assignment prompts. Using shared curriculum is always an administrative concern because it exists in a context of multiple and sometimes competing influences and needs. The development, distribution, maintenance, and administration of shared materials, including their amount and flexibility, depend on the institutional context of the writing program and the needs of its instructors, students, and other stakeholders. In this FAQ, we expand the common conception of shared curriculum (SC), provide a framework for better describing different types of SC, and suggest guidelines for administering SC. This FAQ is organized based on a timeline of SC lifecycle from development to retirement. Your program might have more than one SC initiative in different stages; whether you have used shared syllabi and textbooks for years or might be newly developing open educational resources or assessment-focused assignments, we hope that the questions and answers below will help you navigate the complexities and unique demands of administering your SC projects.

Our Context

In the FAQs below, we draw on our experiences across multiple institutions. Currently, we are WPAs at a large R1 Hispanic-serving institution in the Southwestern U.S., where our writing program employs over 150 instructors (most of whom are renewable contract faculty, none of whom are tenure track) and serves over 7,500 students each year across our main campus, online campus, and multiple international partner campuses. We utilize a variety of SC materials that exist at different stages of their lifecycles: our custom textbook is in its 41st edition, while our Pre-Designed Courses (PDCs) for first-year writing courses have existed since 2015. Over our careers at multiple institutions (with Rochelle having taught nine years at a community college), we both have guided multiple SC projects through their entire lifecycles. Both of us have developed SC materials from scratch and have had to step into robustly developed SC ecologies. Although the majority of examples of WPAs' decisions or processes included in this article come from our experiences working at large R1 universities, we believe that the principles of directing a SC ecology described above can easily apply to other types of institutions and programs. We hope that our readers will be able to adapt our recommendations to their specific contexts.

Acknowledgment of Limitations

While this piece aims to expand how we understand, describe, and work with SC, it does not make claims regarding the efficacy of SC or dismiss many legitimate concerns over expanded use of SC. Rather, we start with the assumption that SC is a fact of life and a necessity for many, if not most, writing programs, and while we offer a more nuanced description of SC and the administrative work it creates, we also call on our field to conduct empirical investigations into the spectrum of SC ecologies and their effectiveness. Such empirical studies exist in the scholarship about online learning, but administrative practices involving SC within broader contexts have not been "examined in any particular depth" (NeCamp & Kendall Theado, 2021, p. 2).

Furthermore, while we describe some important ways student and instructor diversity can impact SC initiatives, we also feel that engaging with relevant literature from a diverse range of scholars in a meaningful and satisfactory way would go well beyond the scope and focus on this article, given its length constraints and its practical orientation. We want to emphasize that addressing racial, linguistic, and cultural diversity in programs with robust shared curriculum ecologies would require its own publication that would center these ideas and explore them in sufficient depth and detail; we hope that by expanding our conversation about SC initiatives, this article will spur more extensive research into this important topic.

What Is Shared Curriculum (SC)?

We use the term "shared curriculum" (SC) to refer to all required or heavily promoted instructional materials. Many writing programs utilize SC materials to create a framework for how a course can or should be taught (NeCamp & Kendall Theado, 2021). Some SC materials like syllabus templates, required textbooks, and instructional materials are so widely used in writing programs that they are rarely labeled as SC, but other forms of SC, such as fully designed online courses, tend to raise more concerns of standardization, academic freedom, or instructor autonomy.

Shared curriculum can play an important role in standardization initiatives, but it does not necessarily lead to wider standardization within a writing program. Although many scholars, like NeCamp and Kendall Theado in *Working With and Against Shared Curricula* (2021), define SC with more of an emphasis on "major assignments" and "overall structures" (p. 2), our experience suggests that SC exists on a sliding scale ranging from institutionally-set course parameters to fully developed online courses (also known as pre-designed or master courses). With this broad understanding of SC, we would argue all writing programs have shared curriculum, even if it is only things like student learning outcomes, required syllabus policies, or a required textbook. Figure 1 represents how every SC component exists along two scales: the amount (or depth) of the materials included and the rigidity or flexibility of adapting the shared materials. For instance, in the bottom left corner are the course parameters set by the institution that are not allowed to be modified: they usually include the course description, learning outcomes, the mode of instruction, and duration of class meeting times. These parameters might define what a course is, but they provide little instructional support; the course is left "with so little curricular shape that it is scarcely the same class" (Gilfus, Conrey, & Nappa-Carroll, 2021, p. 62) from one course section to another. More importantly, it leaves instructors without adequate support as they face the additional labor demands of developing their own curriculum. On the other hand, SC materials such as pre-designed online courses (PDCs) include a large number of instructional materials but may vary widely in terms of how much instructors can modify these materials; some programs limit instructors' ability to alter any part of the curriculum while others allow a high amount of flexibility. Gilfus and colleagues (2021) warned that locking in course curriculum "for the sake of scalability assumes all students and all learning environments are similar enough that a universalized template can be overlaid on every program classroom" (p. 62). We argue that neither extreme is ideal. Providing too few SC materials, flexible or inflexible, can overwhelm instructors and negatively impact program coherence, while a highly developed SC with little flexibility limits instructor autonomy and the ability to cater to specific and diverse student needs.

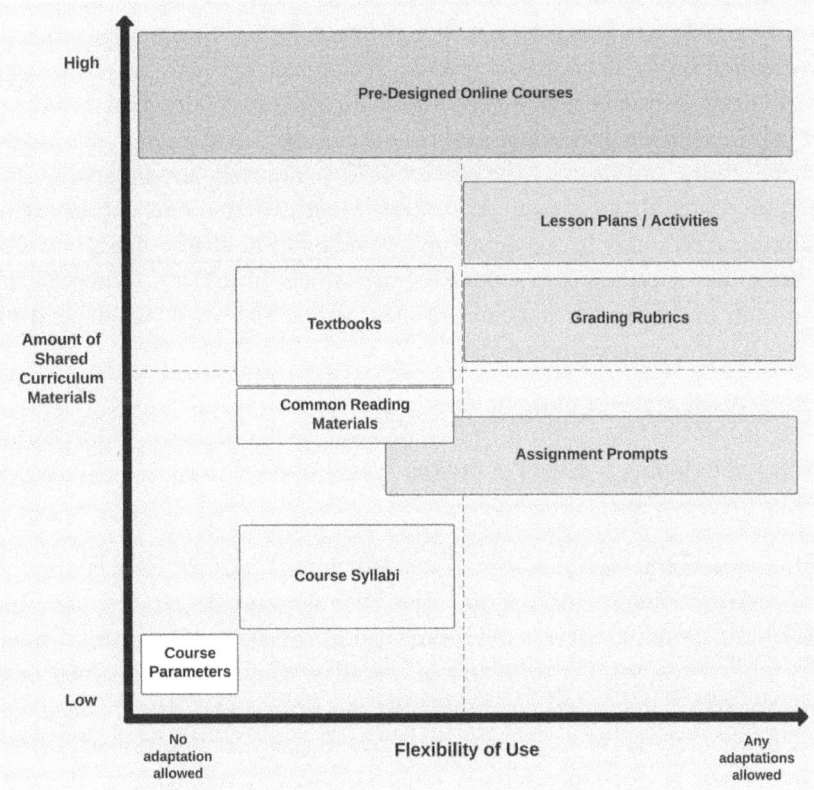

Figure 1. Shared Curriculum Materials Visualization Chart

Stage One: Developing Shared Curriculum

Do I Really Need Shared Curriculum?

The need for SC usually emerges from the need to support instructors who might be new to teaching or new to the specific teaching context, course outcomes, modality, etc. Sometimes it is instructors who have been hired at the last minute, but it can also be instructors who do not have the time or energy (nor are they paid enough) to develop their own materials. Online PDCs, the most heavily developed type of SC, are often used by writing programs as a means to alleviate the heavy burden of online course design (Meloncon & Arduser, 2013; Oblinger & Hawkins, 2006; Rodrigo & Ramírez, 2017).

Administrators, especially at large programs, may share curriculum to standardize or promote policies, pedagogies, or teaching materials. While some may have justified concerns over wider standardization, administrative overreach, or loss of instructor autonomy, there are legitimate reasons to streamline curricular choices. For example, most writing programs have a required textbook because it would not be possible to accommodate every individual instructor's choice of a textbook. Similarly, many programs have a required course portfolio assignment that is part of the program's assessment efforts; in this case, the portfolio SC parameters are dictated by the requirements of the assessment process. Finally, shared curriculum might support instructors in the adoption and adaptation of new curricular initiatives like socially just teaching and assessment practices. Ultimately, the decision to use SC (or not) and its exact scope and form will depend on your specific context and needs.

Whose Needs Do I Need to Consider?

When developing a new SC initiative, you will need to consider the needs of its users as well as stakeholders.

SC users. There are two main intended user groups for SC. First, in a non-Machiavellian sense, it is instructors who need the support. The adjunctification of the contemporary neo-liberal university, a trend we've felt in first-year writing programs for decades, is intricately entwined with the use of SC in writing programs (NeCamp & Kendall Theado, 2021, p. 4). There are a lot of situations where new instructors might benefit from the support of SC. However, we think most readers will acknowledge that a lot of writing programs, especially large ones, require use of specific syllabus templates and textbooks, independent of the experience and expertise of the instructors. For many SC materials though, their flexibility can vary according to the user base: some materials might be required or heavily suggested for new instructors and GTAs while being only recommended for veteran instructors.

The other intended user group for many SC instructional materials such as syllabi templates, textbooks, assignment prompts, or online activities, is students. Thus, SC development bears the weight of a double audience: promoting instructor use while also considering how students respond to and interact with the materials. At their core, SC materials need to be grounded in sound writing pedagogy and attend to the needs of the specific student populations of a given institution. Students are not a monolithic group; for instance, scholarship discusses the contrast between online and in-person student populations (Darby & Lang, 2019; Moore & Kearsley, 1996) or the needs of linguistically diverse students as they apply to SC initiatives (Amorim & Martorana, 2021). Because SC materials will be reaching a large number of students, it is extremely important that these materials account for and accommodate a diverse range of students' backgrounds and needs. From ensuring accessibility to taking an active anti-racist stand, SC developers have an opportunity to promote equity on a programmatic scale with well-designed SC materials. Developing for both accessibility and equity can be especially important for larger SC initiatives such as PDCs; according to the *CCCC State of the Art of OWI Report* (2021), only 48% of instructors viewed their online courses as ADA compliant, and only 37% tried to accommodate their ESL students (p. 11).

SC stakeholders. As WPAs, we often find ourselves at an intersection of the conflicting demands of different stakeholders. "Stakeholders" are other entities within and outside the writing program who might have a stake in the writing program's operations but who are not the intended users of the SC materials. While the needs of our students and instructors should always come first, other examples of stakeholders who might have a say in how SC materials need to be developed or distributed include the following:

- bookstore representatives;
- textbook publisher representatives and editors;
- instructional designers;
- instructional technology support staff; and
- representatives from other campus units (advisors, registrars, general council, etc.).

These stakeholders' agendas might not always align well with the goals or values of the writing program. For instance, syllabi often represent institutional, sometimes even regional, policies and values that can be difficult to align with those of the writing program (Poblete, 2014). The WPA acts as a negotiator between stakeholders to maintain SC's pedagogical integrity while also meeting larger contextual requirements. Describing standardization efforts at her institution, Carter-Tod (2007) urges us to strive towards writing program standards "that operate at a subversive level by returning authority to the individuals teaching in our writing programs as well as to individual student writers, all the while meeting the agenda and goals of the larger institution" (p. 77). A SC needs to serve its users first and foremost, and, to paraphrase Gilfus et al. (2021), it is the WPA's role to amplify the instructors' and students' voices in the fight.

Who Should Develop SC Materials?

In an ideal scenario, developing a shared curriculum (SC) is a transparent process that includes all users and stakeholders. More realistically, however, you will want to have a group of instructors involved in the design process, and you will need to ensure that this group includes diverse instructor voices representing different academic, cultural, and linguistic backgrounds, professional and personal experiences, and levels of teaching expertise. Inviting and actively seeking out input from diverse instructor voices will help make the SC design process "more functional" (Fulford, 2011) and provide a space where divergent perspectives on curriculum and pedagogy can be negotiated and reconciled; moreover, it will ensure larger buy-in for the new SC implementation. For example, our shared syllabus template is managed by a program committee made up of representatives from our different instructor groups. At some point, however, you might find yourself (as we have in the past) in circumstances where you have to develop an entire online course or a new syllabus template with little faculty or student input. In such cases, you will need to collect and implement feedback from a diverse group of both instructors and students as part of the revision process. Developing more robust SC materials (those higher on the vertical axis) may require involving other developers, such as instructional, web, or visual designers (van Rooij & Zirkle, 2016; Oblinger & Hawkins, 2006). Such support can be tremendously helpful; however, it also invites more stakeholders who might have a different vision or agenda for the SC. In our past experiences, not all instructional designers had sufficient background in writing pedagogy, and some wanted to introduce elements that would serve larger university-wide standardization initiatives but not necessarily improve instructor or student experience with writing courses.

How Do I Distribute SC Materials?

It is one thing to have materials ready to share; it is another to get said materials to the people who need them. So much of this process is now digital, including textbooks. Many shared curricular materials are distributed through file sharing environments like Google Drive or Box as well as sharing materials through a learning management system (LMS).

What used to be simply giving a hard copy of the textbook to a newly hired instructor can now be constrained by the digital systems' requirements. For example, a new instructor might have to be officially "in the system" before you can give them access to your digital textbook—which can be difficult with last-minute hires or with an overwhelmed HR office. It is important to think of alternative distribution channels; for example, you might get access codes from your publisher to let new instructors access the textbook ahead of time or share access to your program's SC materials via an online platform that does not require an institutional login. For example, we share our programs' materials through Google Drive and via a website outside of our institution's LMS.

Who Owns the SC?

When shared curriculum is either derived from something else (like syllabi templates from central administration) or collaboratively developed by people in the program, it is usually easier to make the argument that the program owns the curricular material. However, when one or a few individuals do the initial build, who owns the curriculum—the individuals, the program, the larger institution? We have found that regardless of what the institutional policy says (be sure to look for your institution's policy or check with your Office of General Council—the lawyers!), it is easiest to give credit where credit is due. For example, our online PDCs have kept track of who has done the major building and revision work. Those names are included in the instructor user manuals developed for each course, although they are not visible to our students. We prompt instructors who have provided significant content and labor to claim the work as part of their service load and to put it on their CV.

STAGE TWO: GROWING PAINS

How Do I Promote SC Usage?

For optional SC materials, promoting them might look as simple as sharing them via an online platform and informing instructors of their availability. In our experience, novice instructors or those new to the writing program are typically grateful and adopt these materials widely. More experienced instructors might appreciate SC materials if they seek to diversify their instruction or teach a new course (or quickly transition to remote learning during a pandemic!).

For required SC materials, the need for positive promotion becomes more acute as many instructors may resist required curricular materials. Just as students want to understand how and why an assignment improves their writing, instructors require the same understanding for any SC in the program. This includes external factors, such as assessment requirements, that may drive the use of a specific type of SC.

SC materials and the WPAs promoting them need to make very clear how the materials benefit students and instructors. Some questions can be answered through collaborative design and revision processes for SC materials; however, during the initial promotion of SC, WPAs might need to do more to demonstrate how using SC can benefit instructors. For example, as Thompson (2021) points out, they might be able to focus on "teaching goals that would be impossible to achieve if they had to design the basic content" (p. 86), such as providing more extensive individualized feedback to students. Furthermore, it will help alleviate instructors' concerns or feelings of resistance if they can see clearly enough how much flexibility SC materials allow and where and how they might be adapted. In our online program, instructors teaching online for the first time must use the PDC as is, but after their first online course, they are encouraged to adapt the materials based on their strengths and past experience with the courses. Finally, in order to promote wider adoption, WPAs can stress that the SC materials promote higher teaching standards, whether in terms of accessibility, more advanced pedagogical approaches, or addressing the needs of your institution's specific student demographics.

How Do I Support SC Usage?

Promoting and supporting the use of shared materials require that instructors understand how and why the materials are used. For some materials, like syllabus templates, you might be able to add comments with guidelines directly on the documents. More robust SC materials will require more extensive guidelines. For example, our PDCs come with an instructor manual that includes a task-by-task overview of the curriculum as well as general recommendations for teaching online.

In addition to the built-in support guidelines that accompany SC materials, our WPA team offers individual support opportunities at crucial points in the semester, such as drop-in online and in-person support hours for setting up their course materials at the beginning of the semester or support sessions for using the portfolio prompt towards the end of the semester.

Supporting instructors' ability to adapt SC materials, especially in an LMS, can be complicated. Sharing a PDC requires developing a procedure that would define whether instructors can choose to use the entire PDC, use only some parts of it, or have the PDC content automatically uploaded into their individual course shells. Similarly, the flexibility of use for a given PDC will depend not only on the writing program policy but also on how easily instructors can navigate the LMS. The difficulties instructors might face in adapting the PDCs can create the perception of its inflexibility and spur feelings of resentment. In such cases, proactive technology support becomes necessary, such as offering instructors resources or trainings for how to make SC materials work within the LMS or other digital tools.

Sometimes constraints provide opportunities to have difficult discussions. One way to support faculty that are required to use SC is to provide spaces to have discussions about where and how the SC is, or is not, accessible or allows instructors to adopt and adapt anti-racist pedagogies. One of Rochelle's favorite memories of implementing a PDC at the community college was the fact that the discussions did not focus on what button to push: instead, it was three hours of discussion on "why did you design it that way?" These types of discussions also allow for faculty and administrators to distinguish between design and delivery (Rodrigo & Mitchum, 2023, p. 37) as ways to open up assumed inflexibility of use.

How Do I Guide SC Usage?

Once shared curriculum starts to settle, you need to develop some guidelines or policies about how it is used. New instructors will want to know if they are required to use the SC. Instructors who have used your SC before will want to know if they must keep using it, how much they can change it, and when and how it is revised.

One aspect of policy we have always struggled with is the "how much can I change?" question. Trying to articulate what is changeable is difficult. Saying something like "you can only change 30% of a PDC" is meaningless. How do you calculate 30% of curricular material? Try to be as detailed as possible when providing adaptation guidelines. For example, syllabus templates can include ranges for how much specific assignments and attendance can be weighted towards the final calculated course grade.

With more robust SC materials such as PDCs, more guidelines will be necessary; but more importantly, these materials involve more stakeholders that often bring more complicated usage and adaptation restrictions. For example, our online campus (Arizona Online) uses the Quality Matters rubric to ensure our online courses follow the best practices in online learning; however, that also means that our instructors teaching Arizona Online courses are not allowed to make significant changes to the PDCs (Mitchum & Rodrigo, 2021). One way to work around this limitation is to give instructors more autonomy over the curriculum by offering multiple options. For instance, our PDCs for English 101 and 102 come with built-in alternative assignments that instructors can choose from. Offering too many options can create unnecessary work for instructors who may have to make numerous curricular decisions without prior knowledge of the distinctions between the options. More autonomy in adopting and adapting the SC provides space for more expansive use by diverse instructors and students.

How Do I Revise SC Materials?

Your shared curriculum will change! Institutions will change syllabus policies. Textbook companies will update a book. Technology interfaces will get upgraded, or old links to external resources will stop working. Much like a living organism, your SC ecology will need constant attention. The WPA's role as the SC supervisor means you are responsible for ensuring your SC materials are updated timely and efficiently. Some necessary updates might not be labor-intensive but will require ongoing attention, such as ensuring external links work properly and updating them when needed. Other updates might require significant labor, such as curriculum revision after revised course outcomes. Revising too often leads to burnout; not revising enough leads to stale, even outdated, materials. We suggest that if you are not required to make changes due to an update that was out of your control, you should let the changes accumulate and make them all at once during a bulk revision.

Any revision process should involve collecting feedback from instructors and students. For smaller updates, you might implement a simple mechanism such as an online feedback/suggestions survey or an error report form (Mitchum & Rodrigo, 2021). For more extensive or impactful revisions, a more robust and team-based revision process is preferable. For example, we have a Curriculum & Instructional Materials committee that helps oversee the syllabus template and is developing and curating Open Educational Resource (OER) materials. When our program-authored textbook needs revising, a tri-part team made up of a program administrator, a career-track faculty member, and a graduate student instructor edit and author the revised book. The revision process is an opportunity to hear from instructors representing different areas of expertise and different linguistic, cultural, racial/ethnic, or other backgrounds, input which can be even more essential if the initial development did not include diverse perspectives.

How Do I Maintain Materials and Policies?

At this point you might realize that building and maintaining a shared curriculum is a lot of work! We disagree with Pindling et. al.'s (2021) statement that a shared curriculum is a "system meant to reduce administrative workload" (p. 52). In our experience, building, maintaining, and revising SC creates a significant amount of work for WPAs. Initial builds are obviously the most demanding tasks, but WPAs can ask for one-time investments or write proposals for project grants to subsidize the initial build of shared materials (e.g., course releases, stipends). Less obvious is the workload of continued maintenance; as it is often rendered invisible (Rodrigo & Romberger 2021, p. 161), it can be difficult to justify this administrative work with permanent budget lines. Maintaining SC requires both administrative oversight as well as someone who does the labor of making the actual changes.

Sharing this workload with other members of the writing program can help make the maintenance of SC more inclusive, providing opportunities for instructors to share their feedback and have more influence on the SC development as its primary users. Penrose (2012) reminds us that instructor expertise, autonomy, and community are critical to developing professional identity in writing studies, especially with contingent faculty. This work should also be publicly recognized as a valuable contribution to the writing program and the institution. Some of this work can be paid (like course buyouts for editing the new version of the textbook or a grant for socially just pedagogical SC revisions), and some revision work can count as service (like serving on a committee).

If your institution has dedicated units for supporting online or digital instruction, these units might assist with SC revisions either through funding or sharing the workload. However, it is worth noting that accepting help from other units might also mean bringing in more stakeholders who would then have a say in how your SC ecology operates and where it falls along the flexibility and depth axes.

Policies for using shared curriculum, as well as significant changes to our syllabus template, are presented and voted in our program's shared governance processes. Implementing more inclusive and transparent maintenance processes makes everything move more slowly; however, this slow movement is intentional (Berg & Seeber, 2016) and the revisions move at the "speed of trust" (Brown, 2017).

How Do I Introduce Updates?

Just as it is possible to encounter resistance towards SC at the initial implementation stage, updates are met with reluctance as well. Our main suggestions to support updates are these:

1. Warn instructors about the upcoming change as far in advance as possible;
2. Include a clear explanation for why the revisions were necessary; and

3. Whenever possible, provide comparisons between the two versions with descriptions of changes as well as updated user manuals.

If you have the time and resources, especially if the SC is required, ideally provide paid workshop opportunities for instructors to learn about updates.

Stage Three: Maintaining the Program

How Do I Support New and Veteran Instructors?

When using SC materials, especially required textbooks, assignments, or PDCs, many instructors feel like they do not have the autonomy they deserve as professionals. We again invoke Penrose's (2012) emphasis on developing instructor expertise and autonomy as a programmatic goal. We believe both of these goals can coexist with—and be aided by—a SC ecology. Referring back to our SC chart (see figure 1), SC materials should be robust enough to help build instructor expertise and flexible enough not to stifle instructors' autonomy. Participating in the process of revising SC is wonderful professional growth activity and helps build expertise.

As our chart illustrates, much SC material does not exist as a single-pixel dot along the axes; rather, it stretches along the axes and can accommodate a variety of situations and needs. SC can be most beneficial to novice instructors or those new to your specific institutional and programmatic contexts. For more experienced instructors, SC can become optional after they have used it for a while. Many institutions that have graduate students as instructors of record require that graduate students use a specific curriculum for their first year but not after that initial year of teaching. We are the first to confess that we became stronger online instructors once we were designing and developing our own courses. Discussing with instructors when and why a SC is required, desired, or optional, along with strategies to adapt it, is critical. The latter is particularly important as instructors may struggle to envision how to make modifications. WPAs must also continue negotiating with other SC stakeholders outside of the writing program and advocating for more flexibility in their SC materials.

How Do I Transition Administrative Oversight?

Long term SC projects transfer ownership over time. For example, we inherited a custom textbook that has over 40 editions. We are lucky we have copies of almost every edition. Once SC materials become digital, however, the ownership question takes on a new meaning: who owns the digital account(s) that hosts the SC for things like videos, LMS templates, or digital documents? What will happen to these materials if the owner has to leave the institution?

The most important element of transitional administrative oversight is knowing you will need to do it. The mistake is to design and develop anything as if the first designer will always manage the materials. Administrators who oversee SC must design shared and easily transferred materials from the beginning. Email and other accounts that are institutional or group owned, rather than individual, will help with easing the transfer, as well as knowing which materials can have shared ownership and which ones cannot. Furthermore, your writing program will need to have a mechanism in place for introducing new writing program administration team members into the existing SC ecology. Keeping records and designing a WPA handbook can help ease the transition. In addition, when a new administrator joins the team, it is important that they get first-hand experience with the SC materials as users.

How Do I Assess the SC Program?

We now introduce the dreaded A word: assessment. How will you know if your SC is working the way you intend if you are not assessing it? Obviously, it is important to assess how well the SC works for the two primary users, students and instructors. It is also important to occasionally collect feedback from all major stakeholders. For example, to check in with our digital textbook process, we periodically hold meetings that include representatives from the textbook publisher, the digital textbook distributor, our institutional textbook store, and folks who oversee and support our LMS.

Shared curriculum assessment methods can be casual, like end-of-term meetings with online instructors who use PDCs. Or they might be robust, like surveying all online students using PDCs. If your institution requires end-of-term course evaluation surveys, you might be able to add a question or two to those instruments. You don't have to collect data on every element from every stakeholder on an annual basis; you might develop a three- or five-year cycle that collects different types of assessment data over time. The point is to regularly gather data about the use of the SC so that you can revise the SC materials as well as the policies and processes.

How Do I Determine When SC is No Longer Needed?

How do you decide when specific SC materials, policies, or processes need to be significantly revised or retired? Again, it is critical that you are regularly collecting feedback and assessing the program. It is also important that this review process includes all of the SC stakeholders and users. Critical review also requires a careful, systematic review of the programmatic and institutional context as well. Our online PDCs and the policies that surround their use were developed in a time when only a few instructors had online teaching or learning experiences. After the COVID pandemic, we are in a different cultural environment where the vast majority of our writing program instructors have either taught or been students in online environments. At the same time, as LMSs and digital online tools become more advanced or complex, instructors might still benefit from robust but flexible SC materials serving as examples of how to use the LMS or digital tools effectively. Whether or not SC material is needed might also involve negotiating with multiple stakeholders outside of our online writing program. In this process, as at most other points addressed in this FAQ, the primary role of WPAs is to advocate for the needs of the SC users (instructors and students) first and to find compromises whenever SC stakeholders' and/or users' interests might collide.

References

Amorim, Jacqueline, & Martorana, Christine. (2021). Online teaching, linguistic diversity, and a standard of care. In Connie Kendall Theado & Samantha NeCamp (Eds.), *Working with and against shared curricula: Perspectives from college writing teachers and administrators* (pp. 13–28). Peter Lang.

Berg, Maggie, & Seeber, Barbara K. (2016). *The slow professor: Challenging the culture of speed in the academy.* University of Toronto Press.

Brown, Adrienne Marie. (2017). *Emergent strategy: Shaping change, changing worlds.* AK Press.

Carter-Tod, Sheila. (2007). Standardizing a first-year writing program: Contested sites of influence. *WPA: Writing Program Administration, 30*(3), 75–92. https://associationdatabase.co/archives/30n3/30n3carter-tod.pdf

CCCC Online Writing Instruction Standing Group. (2021). *The 2021 state of the art of OWI report.* Conference on College Composition and Communication. https://cccc.ncte.org/wp-content/uploads/2022/05/2021SoAFullReport.pdf

Darby, Flower, & Lang, James M. (2019). *Small teaching online: Applying learning science in online classes.* Jossey-Bass.

Fulford, Collie. (2011). Hit the ground listening: an ethnographic approach to new WPA learning. *Writing Program Administration, 35*(1), 159–162.

Gilfus, Jonna, Conrey, Sean M., & Nappa-Carroll, Melanie. (2021). Rigorous adaptability in the concurrent enrollment writing classroom. In Connie Kendall Theado & Samantha NeCamp (Eds.), *Working with and against shared curricula: Perspectives from college writing teachers and administrators* (pp. 61–74). Peter Lang.

Meloncon, Lisa, & Arduser, Lora. (2013). Communities of practice approach: A new model for online course development and sustainability. In Kelli Cargile Cook & Keith Grant-Davie (Eds.), *Online education 2.0: Evolving, adapting, and reinventing online technical communication* (pp. 73–90). Baywood Publishing Company, Inc.

Mitchum, Catrina, & Rodrigo, Rochelle. (2021). Administrative policies and pre-designed courses (PDCs): Negotiating instructor and student agency. In Connie Kendall Theado & Samantha NeCamp (Eds.), *Working with and against shared curricula: Perspectives from college writing teachers and administrators* (pp. 29–44). Peter Lang.

Moore, Michael G., & Kearsley, Greg. (1996). *Distance education: A systems view*. Wadsworth.

NeCamp, Samantha, & Kendall Theado, Connie. (2021). Working with and against shared curricula: An introduction. In Connie Kendall Theado & Samantha NeCamp (Eds.), *Working with and against shared curricula: Perspectives from college writing teachers and administrators* (pp. 1–12). Peter Lang.

Oblinger, Diana G., & Hawkins, Brian L. (2006). The myth about online course development: "A faculty member can individually develop and deliver an effective online course." *Educause Review, 41*(1), 14–15. Retrieved from http://er.educause.edu/articles/2006/1/the-myth-about-online-course-development

Penrose, Ann M. (2012). Professional identity in a contingent-labor profession: expertise, autonomy, community in composition teaching. *Writing Program Administration, 35*(2), 108–126.

Pindling, Megan, Price, Emily, & Wan, Amy J. (2021). Impossibilities of scalability: Autonomy, adjunctification, and apprenticeship in the age of austerity crisis. In Connie Kendall Theado & Samantha NeCamp (Eds.), *Working with and against shared curricula: Perspectives from college writing teachers and administrators* (pp. 45–60). Peter Lang.

Poblete, Patti. (2014). Battlegrounds and common grounds: First-year composition and institutional values. *Composition Forum, 30*. http://compositionforum.com/issue/30/battlegrounds.php

Rodrigo, Rochelle, & Mitchum, Catrina. (2023). *Teaching literacy online: Engaging, analyzing, and producing in multiple media*. National Council of Teachers of English.

Rodrigo, Rochelle, & Ramírez, Cristina D. (2017). Balancing institutional demands with effective practice: A lesson in curricular and professional development, *Technical Communication Quarterly, 26*(3), 314–328. https://doi.org/10.1080/10572252.2017.1339529

Rodrigo, Rochelle, & Romberger, Julia. (2021). Actors and Allies: Faculty, IT Work, and Writing Program Support. In K. Cole & H. Hassell (Eds.), *Transformations: Change Work Across Writing Programs, Pedagogies, and Practices* (pp. 146–164). Utah State University Press.

Thompson, Hannah. (2021). From Skeptic to believer to advocate: How I came to understand the benefits of shared curricula writing programs. In Connie Kendall Theado & Samantha NeCamp (Eds.), *Working with and Against Shared Curricula: Perspectives from College Writing Teachers and Administrators* (pp. 75–90). Peter Lang Publishing.

Mariya Tseptsura is director of the online writing program at the University of Arizona. Her research interests often bring together writing program administration, online writing instruction, and second language writing. Her work has appeared in *College Composition and Communication* and *Research in Online Literacy Education* as well as multiple edited collections, including *Nonnative English-Speaking Teachers of U.S. College Composition: Exploring Identities and Negotiating Difference* (WAC Clearinghouse, 2024). She has been teaching writing online for over ten years and has been building and directing online shared curriculum initiatives for the past six years.

Rochelle (Shelley) Rodrigo is the WPA and a professor in the Rhetoric, Composition, and Teaching of English graduate program at the University of Arizona. With Catrina Mitchum, Shelley recently co-authored the award-winning *Teaching Literacy Online* (National Council of Teachers of English, 2024) and is working with Susan Miller-Cochran on the fourth co-authored edition of *The Wadsworth/Cengage Guide to Research* (Cengage). In 2021 she was elected Vice President (four-year term including President) of the National Council of Teachers of English and won the Arizona Technology in Education Association's Ruth Catalano Friend of Technology Innovation Award.

Essays

Using a Faculty Survey to Model Successful Instruction in First-Year Writing: Faculty Development Without Faculty Conflict

Liberty Kohn

Abstract

This article explains the use of an anonymous faculty survey of first-year writing instructional practices distributed to all full-time English faculty. The article also describes the subsequent presentation of the survey results to illustrate successful teaching practices and course design to a department where all tenure-line faculty (literature, creative writing, TESOL/linguistics, and rhet-comp) teach first-year writing. The article details the process of using a faculty survey to quantify and produce strong visual data on effective pedagogy and practice, with the survey results standardizing these positive practices during faculty development sessions. Additionally, this article also investigates how my own departmental survey potentially evidences the long-term effectiveness of graduate training of all English PhDs (rhet-comp, literature, linguistics, creative writing, etc.) in process-based pedagogy over the last several decades, even as my survey highlighted some mild differences in pedagogical approach by English subfield, mainly in reading instruction and the use of low-stakes writing.

WPAs influence and are influenced by the local environment: the program history; the relative experience of teachers; the balance of tenure, untenured, and adjunct positions; the amount of autonomy inside the curriculum and in course design; the longevity of contracts; and many other factors that change from institution to institution. WPAs temper these variations to ensure first-year writing meets a department's goals and outcomes.

In small and medium-sized English departments where tenure-line faculty of different subfields (literature, creative writing, rhet-comp, etc.) teach first-year writing, one issue WPAs face is honoring tenure-line autonomy while simultaneously building a program of concentric course design and pedagogy. This article will detail an anonymous survey of teaching praxis taken by tenure-line faculty and full-time instructors and my use of the survey for purposes of assessment and faculty development.

Department and Program Background

I teach in an English department at a public university with approximately seven thousand students. A great majority of the first-year writing courses in my department is taught by tenure-line professors. Of the tenure-line faculty at the time of the survey, fifteen of twenty had PhDs in and strong loyalties to literature, even if several of these literature PhDs also hold an MFA and function largely as creative writing faculty. In addition to this group of fifteen, two faculty had PhDs in rhetoric and composition—this includes me—and three were TESOL/linguistics specialists. All permanent faculty teach two first-year writing courses a year. Additionally, the department employs several instructors in any given academic year to teach up to three sections of first-year writing a semester, four to six graduate students in our literature MA program who each teach a section a semester, and an adjunct or two to teach sections when necessary. An additional historical oddity of our first-year writing curriculum is that we have just one semester of first-year writing, a four-credit course, English 111.

Additionally, no WPA exists in my department. A WPA would have little domain: these autonomous tenure-line faculty teach approximately forty of the fifty to fifty-five sections of first-year writing annually. Due to faculty autonomy, we also have no established or required textbooks or sequence of assignments for first-year writing. Moreover, I am not a WPA, but I am the semblance of a WPA. I do WPA-like things when my department needs them; technically, I am the chair of the department's Composition Committee, but I am not a WPA "in charge" of first-year writing. From a managerial viewpoint, with no WPA to manage first-year writing, my department's first-year writing experience could easily be conceived of as a free-for-all or nightmare waiting to happen. Yet as I'll detail, our first-year writing has consistency in methods and materials, with only a few outliers pertaining mainly to reading instruction rather than writing instruction.

The tenure-line faculty in my department teach first-year writing as at least a third (eight of twenty-four credits) of their teaching load, a situation not unique to my department. Statistics show many departments have tenure-line faculty teaching first-year writing. According to the 2017 National Census of Writing, four-year universities had ninety-five respondents answer they have tenure-line faculty teach 0% of first-year writing, while 125 four-year respondents acknowledged that between 1% and 49% of their classes were taught by tenure-line faculty. Forty respondents answered that tenure-line faculty teach a percentage of first-year writing classes in the broad range between 50% and 100%, with percentages more numerous in the 50–70% range than in the 90–100% range ("What Percentage of

Sections?"). Based on these numbers, we see that a majority of respondents from four-year universities have tenure-line faculty teaching at least some first-year writing. This fact forces many WPAs to navigate the autonomy and privilege of tenure-line faculty who teach first-year writing.

The goal of my first-year writing teaching survey, outlined in this article, was to provide formative data that would allow us to identify program coherence and improve coherence when missing. Along the way, I discovered other uses of the survey data: to norm good teaching, to imply changes to any respondents that were out of line with best first-year writing practices, and to do this without having to summon solely my own expertise or authority as the reason for change. I learned that, skillfully deployed, the positive results of a departmental survey can serve as a non-confrontational framework to discuss first-year writing amongst an autonomous faculty with a variety of doctoral backgrounds and attitudes toward pedagogy and first-year writing.

Assessing the Instruction of a Largely Tenured First-Year Writing Faculty

Because of a WPA's location between students, faculty, and administration, WPAs are on the frontlines of assessment. Yet what and how to assess can be baffling. Melissa Nicholas states that upper administration will often request that a WPA deliver program assessment, yet there is only a mild chance that the WPA has been told by administration "what kind of information they want" (1). Often, goals may be unclear. Thus, the WPA often has the problem of an "amorphous mandate . . . of what to assess and how to assess [which] can be overwhelming" (11). Nicholas calls for a formative, process-based model of assessment (12)—something that points the way toward specific change and a process to do so.

WPAs not only assess student learning but are responsible for tracking the quality of instruction and offering professional development. Libby Barlow, Steven Liparulo, and Dudley Reynolds argue of assessment that "[u]seful results . . . are actionable, and they can be used by those who would be responsible for action" (54). The results toward action—in this case, improved teaching—can help faculty when assessment of student writing alone cannot provide full insight into the cohesion of a program, first-year writing experience, and faculty teaching methods.

The use of formative assessment on teaching practices fits nicely into a larger move in higher education toward outcomes-based assessment. As Michael Carter reports, "we're used to thinking about education in terms of inputs: . . . . We assume that the inputs we provide students will lead to certain outcomes" (268). However, differences in course design or delivery of the curriculum, part of the input, can affect student writing, the output One must examine the instructional delivery of the program, the input, on the individual and group level as an element that affects output, that is, outcomes. Carter suggests of outcomes-based assessment that

> faculty identify the educational outcomes for a program and then evaluate the program according to its effectiveness in enabling students to achieve those outcomes. The main advantage of this outcomes perspective is that it provides data for closing the educational feedback loop, that is, faculty can use the results of program assessment to further improve their programs. (268)

Thus, assessment and improvement rely on student writing, the output, and the coherence of faculty instruction across sections of first-year writing, which is the dynamic input clearly linked to student output.

Yet instruction, the input, can vary widely, even inside routine Graduate Teaching Assistant (GTA) training during graduate school (Mapes, Jacobson, LaMance, and Vogel 67; Cicchino 88). As Amy Cicchino reports, "the teaching preparation that GTAs receive in their doctoral-granting program has impacts that reach beyond the immediacy of [a] graduate-teaching career, having long-term ramifications" (87). Differently trained English PhDs accept teaching positions at new institutions yet bring their old training and disciplinary pedagogies with them. With such differences in pedagogy, a strong case can be made for writing program assessment that captures instruction and curriculum delivery, not just quality of student writing.

How's Our Teaching? Navigating Disciplinary Differences

One of the oldest battles of WPAs, real or imagined, is a pedagogical war between composition and literature, a concern pertinent in my own department where a majority of first-year writing is taught by tenure-line literature faculty. These differences were represented in the pages of *College English* in 1993 through the infamous point-counterpoint of Gary Tate and Erica Lindemann on the content and methods of first-year writing. In this debate Tate represents the sage-on-stage literature professor who lectures and runs a teacher-centered classroom. Lindemann, the composition specialist, represents a student-oriented, process-oriented first-year writing classroom aligned with composition's preferences for active learning, writing as a recursive process, and writing as a college survival skill that should be transferable to other courses. Tate v. Lindemann captures well the (real or imagined) literature and composition duality.

And how real or imagined is this divide now, several decades later? My survey suggests WPAs shouldn't rush to battle with literature faculty. The scant scholarship on mixed departments teaching first-year writing sketches a continuum that runs from outright hostility, to ignorance, to sympathetic misunderstanding, to collaborative vision.[1]

Because teaching first-year writing is often a prerequisite in small departments for literature or non-rhet-comp specialists, teaching duties automatically have the potential to create hostile faculty who are forced to teach composition, harming student progress (Mastrangelo and Decker 61). However, the stereotype of the "hostile literature professor" may no longer be the norm, as "[t]he tenure track faculty members almost certainly respect the need to teach first-year composition and may be good at it, [even as] they probably have not been trained in composition as an academic field" (Kearns 52). In mixed departments such as my own, I find my colleagues would agree with Paula Krebs, who states, "We should find the commonalities with other specialists, for the sake of the English major we all shape" (69). First-year writing is still the most visible function of the English department across the university. A strong repartee between mixed faculty teaching first-year writing strengthens messaging from the English department while building strong first-year writing programs. Moreover, we should doubt the stereotypical framing of the composition/literature divide.

GTA Training as a Remedy for the Lit/Comp Divide?

The 1993 Tate v. Lindemann dialogue is coeval with the slow introduction of GTA composition methods courses during the 1980s and 90s (Tremmel). That is, Tate v. Lindemann coincides with the rapid adoption of first-year writing methods courses for GTAs in English Studies during the 1990s. This near ubiquitous implementation of methods courses was so thorough by the 1990s that methods courses achieved something akin to national policy and were often a topic of discussion in *WPA: Writing Program Administration* (e.g., Latterell; Cogie; Blakemore; Barr Ebest) and in edited collections such as Betsy Pytlik and Sarah Liggett's *Preparing College Teachers of Writing: Histories, Theories, Programs, Practices* and Sally Barr Ebest's *Changing the Way We Teach*. During this period, WPAs got serious about graduate-level professional development and first-year writing training across the US, even if methods of training differed (and may still differ today) from program to program, and no clear study or consensus proves any particular GTA training program better than another (Cicchino 88).

Mastrangelo and Decker argue in a 2020 *ADE Bulletin* that "an increasing number of graduate programs, particularly ones where rhetoric and composition have a strong presence, insist that all graduate students in English have training in composition theory through seminars, teaching practicums, and extracurricular workshop" (61). Recent data would suggest this true. Examination of the 2017 National Census of Writing's Four-Year Institution Survey asked the question of its participants teaching first-year writing, "What types of initial training is (sic) provided [for first-year writing]?" The results show a great majority of graduate students (87%) take an entire course, while other opportunities and/or requirements in teaching composition also exist. Only five graduate students of 113 who took the survey reported having no training, or, one assumes, at least no mandatory training ("What Types of Initial Training?"). If we trace adoption of GTA programs to the 1990s and early 2000s, it's clear that, over the past two decades, rhet-comp has built a dominant, predictable presence of GTA first-year writing methods courses. Why does this matter now? Currently, WPAs can assume that most English PhDs and MAs with degrees outside of rhet-comp in the last twenty-five years (i.e., most faculty today) will have taken a GTA methods course. These GTA courses now provide WPAs with pedagogical and curricular reference points to discuss first-year writing instruction as a national, cross-institutional set of values and practices.

The Usefulness of an Anonymous Survey to Model Good Instruction

For the WPA interested in assessing first-year writing teaching practices across a department, one question looms: How do I track course materials and variety of instruction amongst colleagues of diverse backgrounds? If a majority of first-year writing instructors are autonomous tenure-line faculty, a second question arises: How might I influence or standardize good teaching of first-year writing amongst tenured faculty who aren't obligated to teach first-year writing as composition wishes? I began to answer these questions with my knowledge that most of my colleagues had a semester-long GTA course in grad school that I could refer to when seeking to norm first-year writing instruction. I also answered these questions through a departmental survey, which would highlight best teaching practices from within our own department.[2]

I was curious how our first-year writing courses resembled a "prototypical" first-year writing course and, conversely, how a course might take on qualities of a literature course due to so many literature-based faculty members teaching first-year writing. As the *de facto* WPA, I also wished to influence first-year writing practices and materials without creating any conflict amongst a highly independent, tenured faculty who gets along well, who takes first-year writing seriously, and who can work together to get hard things done on the departmental level. Lastly, I spent time with both my chair and the several member Composition Committee crafting and revising the questions to avoid resistance or offense to my colleagues, all of whom earnestly take up the challenge of first-year writing despite different pedagogical influences and professional interests.

In terms of the survey's local uses, I knew the results could easily be used to frame our first-year writing coherence, while also identifying problems and suggesting interventions. On a scholarly level, I now believe the survey's results also point to another aspect of professional development: the effectiveness of English departments' GTA methods courses since the 1990s. My survey demonstrates that literature and creative writing faculty in my department are clearly using first-year writing teaching methods learned in their graduate school GTA seminar; with no WPA, they are using them because they want to. Thus, concerning national best practices, the adoption of methods seminars in English graduate study since the 1990s and early 2000s has, at least in my department, greatly unified our delivery of first-year writing, even with no WPA.

The Survey

All permanent faculty teaching first-year writing received a survey of mainly multiple choice questions that pertained to the following: types of writing assignments and assignment sequences; types of and amount of reading assigned; number of papers assigned; the relationship between assigned reading and high-stakes writing; the use and forms of low-stakes writing; the use of peer-review workshops, one-on-one student conferences, and ability to revise; and the daily distribution of activities (reading quizzes, reading guides, small group work, lecture, discussion of reading, free writing, practice of modeled writing, etc.). A copy of the survey questions can be accessed by scanning the QR code at the end of this article.[3, 4]

These topics define assessment territory: characteristics of instructors, material conditions, pedagogical strategies, the role of textbooks, teacher preparation and professional development, and identity issues (Yancey 65). One major criterion, by my own thinking, was to see if faculty were running a process-based classroom, regardless of course design. After all, first-year writing classroom materials and instruction can be diverse: the writing process is less linear and more individualized than the prewriting-writing-revising sequence implies (Lindemann, *Rhetoric* 31), and first-year writing classrooms can contain diverse reading experiences and paper topics taken from cultural studies, critical theory, political issues, or discourse communities (Smit 193-195). Since I was seeking a standard amongst these diverse practices, a fair representation of process-based pedagogy for me as WPA was the ability of students to pre-write and draft slowly over several class meetings, workshop papers with other students, conference with an instructor, and have at least one opportunity to revise. The above is a basic description of process pedagogy in scholarly literature (Smit 193) with the major emphasis of process pedagogy falling on revision activities (Koster Tarvers and Moore 109).

Nineteen of twenty-two faculty completed the survey, with a twentieth participant completing approximately half the survey, an apparent anomaly of the technology as I used it. This high response rate is likely due to the earnestness of my colleagues to create a positive first-year writing experience for students and our department. I also benefitted from being invited by the chair to spend our two-hour Assessment Day meeting discussing the results of the survey. This promised two-hour block of time offered a good reason to complete the survey—faculty were going to discuss the results for two hours, so they may as well take the survey. And the two-hour block of time was a key to discussing, rather than me lecturing on, the survey results.

However, to best use the survey to highlight strengths while also addressing inconsistencies or weak practices, I needed to consider how to present the material to the department during the two-hour session. As Nicholas points out of assessment work with tenured faculty, any "apparent 'secrecy' of [a] project" can quickly transform to "political complication" (21). I knew that even in my collegial, practical department, everyone has a tendency to, if not politicize, at least rationalize their teaching methods as effective and meeting guidelines to justify or shield against any undesirable feelings or criticism.

It is worth noting that several faculty members did voice concern during a department meeting where I announced the survey. These faculty felt, if not spied upon, a bit intruded upon. Both the department chair and I reassured faculty that the survey was about providing a decently uniform student experience in a department of great autonomy as well as making sure that we could tell our dean and university that we were holding up our end of the bargain in providing students the basics of academic writing. In short, the survey wasn't a witch hunt, but the collection of evidence of our successful first-year writing program. With this reassurance, we received a 90% survey completion rate.

The Presentation and Discussion of Survey Results

I chose to not go over each survey question during the two-hour presentation. Rather, I wanted to review positive results of important issues to build good will and buffer defensiveness, then shift toward results in which a minority of individuals were likely not preparing and scaffolding instruction for students as much as possible. Because I had used the survey technology Qualtrics, I was prepared to easily display any results in bar graph form if asked.

I began the presentation by reinforcing our group success and displaying the similarities amongst our materials and instruction. I began with types of writing assignments, assignment sequences, and number of formal pages of writing. These were uniform and positively met our departmental goals and outcomes. We averaged three to four major assignments, nearly all of them based in argument, analysis, or research writing with small appearances of narrative-based assignments by some faculty as an initial assignment. We averaged twenty pages of formal writing, and everyone had at least fifteen pages of formal writing.

Concerning the core of process-based pedagogy—feedback and revision—the results registered a strong process-based pedagogy: although several questions were needed (see survey questions 12 and 13) to get an accurate snapshot, all respondents held peer review workshops before final submission of papers. Fourteen faculty members also included one-on-one conferences or instructor feedback; four faculty members mandated revision when necessary (likely when the paper needed significant revision); and two faculty members utilized portfolios.

The survey allowed instructors to tally multiple processes for revision, so the results are affected by the overlap of instructors' multiple policies of revision—for instance, an instructor utilizing portfolios may also be holding one-on-one conferences and using student peer review, allowing them to tally in each category. Nevertheless, all respondents indicate using student peer review workshops, a basic form of process pedagogy. Fourteen instructors (74%) also review the paper and offer feedback through writing or a one-on-one conference before final submission. This means, of course, that approximately a quarter of the respondents (five) do not offer feedback before final submission; however, these faculty may include the four faculty who require revision upon request, or the two faculty who use a portfolio that allows for revision. The survey was too blunt, even with multiple questions on some topics, to fully capture the nuance of what these five faculty members did instead of holding one-on-one conferences or offering feedback prior to final submission.[5]

Although the details of particular instructors remain a bit murky, clearly faculty are adhering to components of process-based pedagogy. To any faculty who were unaware or not practicing early formative feedback and revision opportunities, the above numbers, however imprecise, are an impressive showing of the use of formative feedback, conferencing, and/or revision by a large majority of the department. These numbers themselves are a data-driven way to display how process-based methods dominate first-year writing in our department, regardless of faculty subfield, to any potential holdouts on running a process-based or revision-based classroom.

I next selected reading instruction as a topic of interest for our faculty development session. I discussed the types of books assigned and the amount of reading per week. The survey showed that everyone in the department had books that counted as a "reader"—mainly long non-fiction books or an anthology of essays. Everyone also had some form of a "rhetoric," a textbook outlining the basics of the writing process. I solicited further discussion of textbooks during the two-hour session, hoping that faculty might share the benefits of their rhetoric with each other, as I knew that some faculty had short handbooks that focused as much on grammar and citation as the writing process.

I didn't seek to control this discussion. I hoped that faculty with fantastic rhetorics might advocate for their effectiveness, which they did. When I spoke, I spoke of student needs: students needing student-level models, pre-writing heuristics, and similar process-based textbook fare that might be absent if faculty were using skill-and-drill handbooks as their "rhetoric." I let faculty discuss how better rhetorics had process components that guided students through the creation of an argument. In this way, faculty coached each other to try something new if necessary. I chimed in at times to re-focus the discussion on particular student needs.

Softening Resistance During Faculty Development

Effective teaching practices, even when evidenced by scholarship on teaching and learning, can be called into question quickly. Although I expected no (and received no) negative comments with my English colleagues, I continuously used survey data to influence good instruction in important or problematic areas. I would begin discussion of a topic by showing the survey question along with its visually represented answer (bar graph). After reading the question, I would standardize the positive answers, kindly note any problematic outliers, then acknowledge the difficulty of a multiple-choice question capturing the complexity of an issue. Next, I would solicit comments from colleagues doing good work in these areas.

For example, my leading of discussion sounded like this: "Next, we have the question 'How many of your assignments require the use of documented sources external to a course text?'" Then, I would load the following slide:

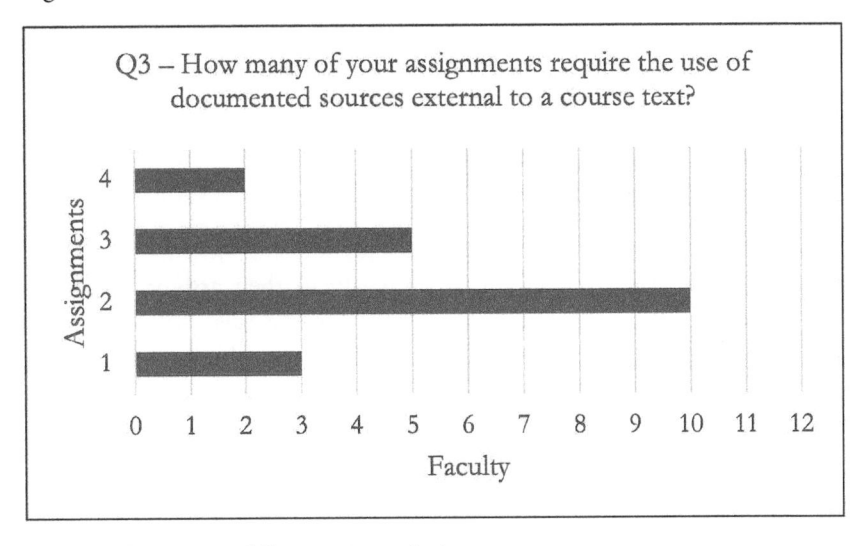

Figure 1. Documented Sources in an Assignment

I would continue,

> Just looking over a snapshot of our work as a department, we might say that a large majority of us believe that at least two assignments should require secondary sources. The data shows that a few of us require secondary sources for only one assignment. Mary, I know your course requires sources early, at least by the mid-point of the semester. I'm wondering if you could tell me why you design your course this way—and maybe how you scaffold and layer source use across your course.

After letting "Mary" explain her course for a few minutes, with my own comments minimal, standardizing my own goals as they arrived in Mary's answer, I might next give "Barbara" the floor, with a slightly different question emphasizing early source use: "Barbara, I know you have an interesting place you like to see students finish in their research and source use at the end of the semester. Could you tell us what it is and how you scaffold source use early in the semester to get them there?"

My main goal was to have others advocate for the topic under discussion. I'd also note my purposeful avoidance of concentrating on the three colleagues who required sources in only one paper. Change doesn't come through statements eliciting shame, blame, or incorrectness (with faculty or students in one's trust); moreover, it is hard to know exactly how secondary texts may appear in my colleagues' courses. I found it important to leave a non-accusatory space for faculty to discuss their own teaching, whatever its form. A WPA shouldn't rush to assumptions here. Norming the positive practices of the majority, in this case a large majority, is a great way to suggest change for those who are open to it.

Addressing Disciplinary Differences: Reading Instruction and Materials

We next shifted into reading instruction, one area where the department also shared a fair amount of similarity in their assigned readings, but an area that I found potentially problematic because, across answers, the majority of the faculty had a general pattern of assigning novel-length works of non-fiction or fiction with a paper due after each, even if the largest survey category included short works with the long work. Here, the data masked as much as it revealed: how exactly were these short works being incorporated by faculty? How much argument, not narrative, existed in the long works faculty preferred? In this case, the data pointed to the need for an important discussion in the undervalued area of reading instruction and the reading-to-write process.

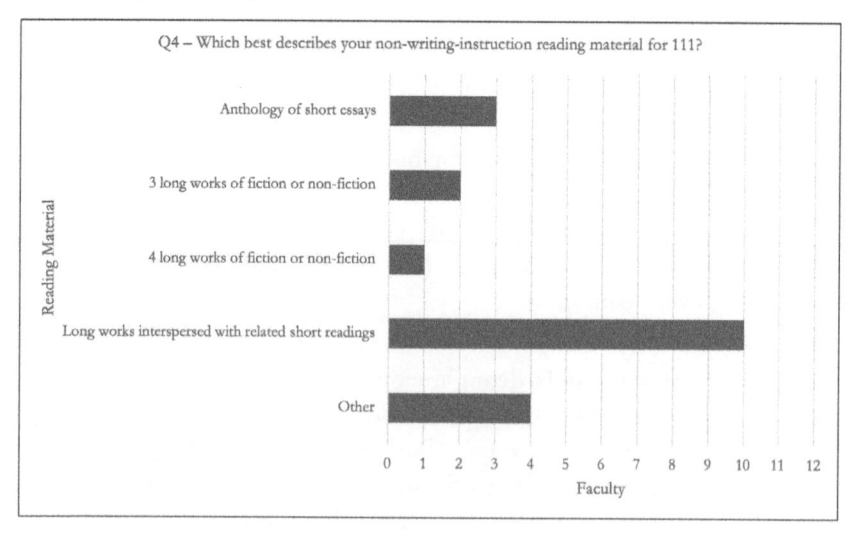

Figure 2. Non-writing Instruction Reading Material

This method of reading instruction and reading-to-write based in long works is different than many first-year writing experiences, in which students are typically exposed to a variety of genres and have mainly short, anthology-based readings with perhaps a long work. Additional to this data about long primary readings, sixteen faculty members did require additional scholarly sources for at least two, if not three or four, of their writing assignments, to create intertextuality. However, three respondents required external scholarly sources for only a single paper (see figure 2). I made sure to note this majority emphasis on multiple source-based assignments to allow us to discuss how faculty were (hopefully) creating intertextuality and synthesis as well as modeling argument when working mainly with a primary text of novel-length.

I spent my time focusing on the reading and reading-to-write process, which are areas where the literature-heavy background of the faculty tipped the department away from the typical reading materials of first-year writing. Using the survey, I wanted to again let faculty discuss how they were teaching reading and how they were connecting reading (and multiple texts) to their writing assignments. I once again advocated for my concerns: teaching multiple genres, including short and long readings, and not having all papers simply be an interpretation of a book of fiction or non-fiction. Both primary and secondary sources can be used many ways, and papers that consistently ask for a response or interpretation of a sole text limit the forms of synthesis that could be experienced in first-year writing.

When I spoke of reading, I pointed out the challenges of gaining multiple perspectives on an issue if reading only a long work of non-fiction (or fiction) that may provide limited counterargument or alternative viewpoints. However, to support the importance of variation in reading-to-write, I plumbed my colleagues' materials and instruction for positive examples. A share of faculty assigned shorter readings that did introduce alternative perspectives on their long non-fiction readings, and I channeled the discussion as I could to let these faculty discuss the reasons why they chose a mixture of readings as opposed to a single long text. Their reasons aligned with introducing counterargument more easily or visibly, seeing texts as in discussion with each other, and providing more genres and different reading experiences. Again, I only brought up the salient issues, suggesting that students might benefit from reading multiple genres or a reading process that required new forms of synthesis in ongoing assignments. My own discussion prompts sounded something like, "When teaching long works of novel length, what do you all do to ensure genre diversity and genre awareness when a long work may not provide it? And what aspects of genre and the uses of short texts in first-year writing does the survey question not capture?" I cued discussions amongst faculty to express how they were achieving these reading goals in the classroom, and perhaps have those who teach just one long text per paper silently ponder any absences in reading instruction or materials and also ponder the benefits of short, non-literary texts to supplement reading instruction.

Using the Survey Data to Suggest Change: Reading

The discussion of reading materials prompted debate about reading instruction, which is symptomatic of an absence of discussion of college-level reading instruction in rhetoric and composition (Sullivan 233; Odom n.p.). The survey showed most members of the department assigned forty to seventy pages of reading per week of content reading. However, several faculty members were once again outliers, with three assigning eighty to one hundred pages a week (see figure 4), likely too much for students to read closely in a class that meets just twice a week, especially if reading from a "rhetoric" was also being assigned.

Two faculty members assigned only ten pages a week, likely too little. I highlighted the department norm and outliers. The ensuing discussion of reading instruction created the greatest difference of opinion amongst faculty, mainly about how students learn to read, and how to work with students who, as one colleague put it, "don't like to read anymore." Moreover, the above data are helpful because no one tells you in graduate school how much reading to assign, even as "everyone knows" writing three papers a semester is typical. The survey helped us explore standards and practices toward this unanswered question of how much reading to assign.

From this question, I also learned that a portion of faculty members believe that students will learn to read better by simply having more assigned reading—more pages equal more practice reading; it follows that these faculty wished to assign a maximum number of pages. I played devil's advocate here, suggesting that students would also benefit from reading shorter, controlled pieces that allow them to practice multiple and specific reading strategies introduced by the instructor. (Not to mention that students may not be reading the overwhelming amount of assigned pages, therein not improving reading comprehension, a point I left to my colleagues to say aloud.) Additionally, approximately 40–50% of students at my institution are first-generation students who work part-to-full time, and the amount of reading expected of students may depend upon an individual student body's characteristics and time constraints, an additional programmatic factor for discussion.

I framed my concerns through composition research on transfer and metacognition by stating that "discussion" of a text doesn't equate to drawing out a replicable, transferable reading strategy—that is, instructors often utilize "discussion" of a reading without clear goals or clear modeling of reading methods or strategies (Joliffe 478). I knew that research demonstrates students are often unclear on how to monitor their reading, but that successful readers are aware of their strategies (Baker and Beall 384). I paraphrased reading guru David Joliffe, who argues, "Students have to read in college composition, but seldom does anyone tell them how or why they should read" (474). Awareness of reading strategy and targeted reading skills are likely better; thus, the assumptive pedagogy of "assigning a lot of pages" was beneficial to discuss with my colleagues, and I suggest that questions probing reading instruction would benefit any survey of faculty teaching practices.

I also wanted to strongly advocate for texts that might serve as a model of the academic style, length, and genre that students would be asked to write. I knew from the survey that 74% of the department (fourteen respondents) used past students' writing as models. Others used professional models, and only two respondents provided no models, which I termed in the survey "I believe students learn best through experimentation, not example." With fourteen of my colleagues utilizing student models, I argued for providing professional and student argument models: studies show that students tend to replicate in their own writing the genre they read—for instance, students write in a more narrative style when offered only narrative readings (Grabe 252), a potential problem if using narrative to teach argument. Thus, reading models of argument, not solely fiction or literary non-fiction, are important inclusions in a first-year writing course, a point I wanted my colleagues to discuss, as many of them are literature specialists with a potential default toward literary pedagogy and long narratives.

Using the Survey Data to Suggest Change: Low-Stakes Writing

The survey showed three faculty members were not having students do low-stakes writing outside of class, and two faculty were not having students do writing during class, leaving student reading and invention relatively unsupported. I made sure to highlight this result. When I put the bar graphs on the screen for the questions about low-stakes writing, I said,

> The survey shows that sixteen of us have students perform low-stakes writing outside of class. Only three of us do not. Also, seventeen of us have students produce writing routinely during class time. You can see we have a strong faculty preference here in what we believe

students need. Students are likely more prepared for classroom tasks and papers because of this practice of writing outside of and inside the classroom.

This was, of course, my way of norming low-stakes writing to the several anonymous instructors that appeared to not have any low-stakes "practice" or reflective writing prior to major papers.

I didn't draw attention to these anonymous faculty members after their initial mention, whoever they were. I did use phrases that, because of the large majority who were using low-stakes writing outside and inside the classroom, confirmed how much we must believe low-stakes writing helps students. I again solicited some discussion on why people felt low-stakes writing was important and what forms they used in their own teaching: this included out-of-class journals, in-class freewriting, reading responses, and similar fare. In what was one of the best moments of the session, one senior faculty member raised his hand and said, "I'm one of those people who doesn't have students write outside of class. I had no idea that everyone was doing that. We didn't do that when I was an undergraduate." The faculty member was simply unaware of how many of his colleagues, regardless of departmental subfield, used various forms of low-stakes writing previous to class to set up everyday classroom activities. He promised to take all recommendations to heart.

Letting Colleagues Select Best Practices

After spending an hour discussing select survey data to reinforce or explore our first-year writing instructional practices, I switched to a different strategy for the second hour. Faculty had been asked to print out their high-stakes writing assignments and organize them in sequence. I had faculty break into groups of four, share their sequences and assignments, then nominate one set of assignments as a shining example of a first-year writing course that addresses all goals and outcomes while providing well-rounded reading and writing experiences that satisfied our English 111 outcomes and goals. My goal in this activity was to have the department, not myself, standardize effective materials and instruction.

This collaborative small group activity was borrowed from WAC workshops I had run, in which faculty members (typically of different disciplines in WAC) read each other's assignments to identify points of confusion as a reader/interpreter of the assignment. In WAC settings, this allows for faculty to read a colleague's assignments from a novice's perspective, pointing out confusions. The idea is that faculty may blame students as poor interpreters of assignments but are less willing to blame colleagues for being poor interpreters of their assignment. In my first-year writing faculty development setting, my goal was to have faculty select strong first-year writing materials based upon the norms identified in our first hour together, then share to create positive social pressure.

This second hour went well, with several groups nominating one sequence, then explaining the sequence and scaffolding. Nothing highly ineffective or problematic arose during this activity; all assignments passed the muster of this informal departmental review. One group, however, resisted choosing a "best" sequence, instead stating that all courses were exemplary—they didn't wish to pick winners and losers. Despite this egalitarian stance that championed while simultaneously resisting, the activity achieved its goal: the department shared with each other strong sequences of first-year writing and vetted or discussed any potentially confusing or poorly constructed assignments through informal Q&A in small groups.

Final Thoughts on Surveying Instructional Methods and Working with Faculty of Diverse Expertise

The survey served as a fantastic tool to avoid my own imposition as the "writing police" amongst my many colleagues (friends) with English PhDs in a variety of subfields. The survey and two-hour session reserved my expertise, allowing tenured literature (and creative writing and TESOL) faculty to share their strong first-year writing pedagogy, therein standardizing good first-year writing instruction from those of differing areas of specialization in the department. The use of a survey placed me as only a messenger, not the expert or gatekeeper. Yet I clearly had an agenda—one that was likely apparent to all. I offset this highly apparent agenda by selecting faculty members that I knew had strong sequences and practices. This offered superb examples of course designs and practices while simultaneously offering positive, bottom-up social pressure if necessary.

I have several basic suggestions for WPAs who wish to use a first-year writing survey. These suggestions are particularly helpful for those WPAs in departments of tenure-line, autonomous faculty who teach first-year writing:

- Selectively use surveys, not solely your expertise, to norm and promote good writing instruction.
- Solicit faculty input and leadership from literature/creative writing faculty (or other non-composition faculty) who are teaching writing well.

- Remember that reading in first-year writing is a wild card that can change course design; don't forget to include reading instruction in faculty development.
- Surveying faculty on teaching practices (not just student output) can provide data useful to various forms of internal and external assessment.

As a caveat, or perhaps a fifth bullet point, I would include that my department's decently high adherence to a process-based classroom may be dependent upon several factors unique to our department demographic and culture, but that align with my earlier claim that most English PhDs will now, in 2024, have had a semester of GTA first-year writing training that WPAs can use to advantage in mixed departments. This early GTA training is another "voice," or form of evidence, or representation of good teaching to be drawn on by WPAs, a voice that is not one's own, but still a rhet-comp colleague's, even if temporally distant.

I'd like to close this article by briefly opining on how any WPA survey emphasizes some elements of teaching and first-year writing programming, while pushing others to the margin; such is true of my own survey that I inherited, revised, and will seek to revise again in light of anti-racist pedagogy. Looking at the survey now, considering the pressing need for anti-racist pedagogy and curriculum, I can see that first-year writing surveys also offer an opportunity to capture and discuss how anti-racist pedagogies are extant in one's first-year writing program. Tyler S. Branson and James Chase Sanchez argue that "the most important antiracist policy recommendation that programs need to change is in curriculum development" (72); moreover, as they report regarding survey data from their own research on writing programs, "respondents indicated that strategies for combating racism in writing programs happened more or less at the individual level as opposed to extending out of explicit, formalized practices" (72). Thus, in addition to materials, design, and process pedagogy, first-year writing surveys should include questions to gather data and capture best practices on anti-racist pedagogy at the individual level and move it to the programmatic level.[6]

In Memoriam

I would like to dedicate this article to my dear friend and colleague Dr. Ethan Krase (1972–2023). Our offices were just a few steps apart for fourteen years, and we traveled together across stretches of time and space more than once in the name of composition. I miss him, and I believe Ethan would find it humorous and heartwarming that he appears in this article under the mysterious pseudonym "department chair."

QR Code Link to Survey Instrument: http://bit.ly/kohn-survey-questions

Notes

1. Most of this scholarship, as an early reviewer of this article pointed out, has appeared mainly in rhet-comp journals, a problem, but still not a reason to suspect a war or resistance with colleagues in literature.

2. Even before my arrival in 2009, my department had a history of distributing a first-year writing survey of several dozen questions to all permanent faculty on their teaching practices. The survey was (and remains) both anonymous and voluntary. Faculty are free to share their teaching practices through several dozen mainly multiple-choice questions; during early discussion of the survey during department meetings, I am always sure not to lead or judge by discussing correct or incorrect teaching practices. This neutrality limits resistance by tenure-line faculty to voluntarily taking the survey. I want (and need) to create an atmosphere of non-judgement when we gather data for critical reflection as an organization, as well as data for any external auditors over the forthcoming years. Based upon my department chair's suggestion, I decided to revive a teaching methods survey. I kept many questions from past departmental surveys while also revising the survey to investigate types of instruction and issues related to a student-centered, process-based classroom common to rhet-comp and, I must admit, my own disciplinary biases and practices.

3. I did not survey and assess graduate students and adjuncts as part of this project so that I could get clearer data on permanent faculty only. I observe and mentor graduate students separately as part of a professional development program

once they begin teaching during their second semester of their MA, just after completing their GTA first-year writing pedagogy course.

4. A survey can also track faculty attitudes toward students. Unfortunately, surveys written before my joining of the department contained questions and answers that allowed faculty to, at least indirectly, blame students for being poor writers. I re-structured any attitudinal frameworks so that faculty must assess student learning difficulties based upon students' educational experience, non-educational experiences, and the cognitive and social difficulty of transitioning to college-level work, as opposed to faculty wishing for likely fictional, idealized differently abled students.

5. I did my best to offset these uncertainties by offering another non-intrusive category of revision, "only prior to submission." Only seven respondents tallied this as a response; thus, twelve respondents allow for revision after grading. Again, there is uncertainty, but with a survey allowing for a variety of options, I have to believe that even the 5 faculty members not reviewing papers before submission are likely providing feedback and revision elsewhere, through either a paper-by-paper basis (four respondents), through portfolio (two respondents), or through the ability to revise after an initial grade is given (twelve respondents).

6. As Branson and Sanchez suggest, the "premise of such an exercise is not that mandating diversity changes attitudes. It often doesn't. However, it does reflect the values of the program" (72), and any surveying of teaching practices should invite data toward understanding of anti-racist programming, especially when there "is a lack of literature on race and WPA work" (71). Despite this lack of literature, questions may begin by probing "alternative counterpublics . . . where literacy is associated with ethnolinguistic diverse communities" (Garcia de Mueller and Ruiz 22), why white respondents and respondents of color differ greatly in their "rat[ing of] institutional strategies as effective" (27) in responding to the "intersection of race and linguistic diversity," and how to move beyond methods where "student support only means a recognition of diverse groups, and reduces support to special groups and lectures" (29). A first-year writing survey that targets anti-racist teaching practices is a tool to begin productive discussion of support for students and faculty of color.

Works Cited

Baker, Linda and Lisa Carter Beall. "Metacognitive Processes and Reading Comprehension." *Handbook of Research on Reading Comprehension*, edited by Susan E. Israel and Gerald G. Duffy, Routledge, 2009, pp. 373–88.

Barlow, Libby, Steven P. Liparulo, and Dudley W. Reynolds. "Keeping Assessment Local: The Case of Accountability Through Formative Assessment." *Assessing Writing*, vol. 12, 2007, pp. 44–59.

Barr Ebest, Sally. "The Next Generation of WPAs: A Study of Graduate Students in Composition/Rhetoric." *WPA: Writing Program Administration*, vol. 22, no. 3, 1999, pp. 65–84.

—. *Changing the Way We Teach: Writing and Resistance in the Training of Teaching Assistants.* Southern Illinois UP, 2005.

Blakemore, Peter. "An Intentionally Ecological Approach to Teacher Training." *WPA: Writing Program Administration,* vol. 21, no. 2/3, 1998, pp. 137–49.

Branson, Tyler S. and James Chase Sanchez. "Programmatic Writing Approaches to Antiracist Writing Program Policy" *WPA: Writing Program Administration,* vol. 44, no. 3, 2021, pp. 71–76.

Carter, Michael. "A Process for Establishing Outcomes-Based Assessment Plans for Writing and Speaking in the Disciplines." *Assessing Writing: A Critical Sourcebook,* edited by Brian Huot and Peggy O'Neill, NCTE/Bedford St. Martins, 2009, pp. 268–86.

Cicchino, Amy "A Broader View: How Doctoral Programs in Rhetoric and Composition Prepare Their Students to Teach Rhetoric and Composition." *WPA: Writing Program Administration,* vol. 44, no. 1, 2020, pp. 86–106.

Cogie, Jane. "Theory Made Visible: How Tutoring May Effect Development of Student-Centered Teachers." *WPA: Writing Program Administration,* vol. 21, no. 1, 1997, pp. 76–84.

Garcia de Mueller, Genevieve. and Iris Ruiz. "Race, Silence, and Writing Program Administration: A Qualitative Study of U.S. College Writing Programs." *WPA: Writing Program Administration,* vol. 40, no. 1, 2016, pp. 19–39.

Grabe, William. "Narrative and Expository Macrogenres." *Genre in the Classroom: Multiple Perspectives,* edited by Ann M. Johns, Routledge, 2001, pp. 249–67.

Jolliffe, David A. "Learning to Read as Continuing Education." *College Composition and Communication,* vol. 58, no. 3, 2007, pp. 470–94.

Kearns, Michael. "The Composition Teacher-Scholar in the New University." *ADE Bulletin,* vol. 137, Spring 2005, pp. 50–56.

Koster Tarvers, Josephine and Cindy Moore. *Teaching in Progress: Theories, Practices, and Scenarios.* 3rd ed. Pearson-Longman, 2008.

Krebs, Paula. "One of Each: The Small College Multi-plex English Department." *ADE Bulletin,* vol. 137, Spring 2005, pp. 67–69.

Latterell, Catherine G. "Training the Workforce: An Overview of GTA Educational Curricula." *WPA: Writing Program Administration,* vol. 19, no. 3, 1996, pp. 7–23.

Lindemann, Erika. "No Place for Literature." *College English,* vol. 55, no. 3, 1993, pp. 311–16.

—. *A Rhetoric for Writing Teachers.* 4th ed. Oxford UP, 2001.

Mapes, Aimee C., Brad Jacobson, Rachel LaMance, and Stefan M. Vogel "Troublesome Knowledge: A Study of GTA Ambivalence with Genre-Informed Pedagogy" *WPA: Writing Program Administration,* vol. 43, no. 2, 2020, pp. 66–88.

Mastrangelo, Lisa and Sharon Decker. "When Literature Faculty Members Must Teach Composition: The Need for Chair-Director Collaboration." *ADE Bulletin,* vol. 158, 2020, pp. 59–70.

National Census of Writing. "What Percentage of Sections of Face-to-Face FYC Were Taught by FT, Tenure-line Faculty in the English Department?" *National Census of Writing,* 2017. https://writingcensus.ucsd.edu/survey/4/

year/2017?question_name=s4y2017fyw22&op=Submit#results. accessed 23 July 2023.

—. "What Types of Initial Training is Provided?" *National Census of Writing*, 2017. https://writingcensus.ucsd.edu/survey/4/year/2017?question_name=s4y2017fyw22&op=Submit#results. accessed 23 July 2023.

Nicholas, Melissa. "Not Sure Where to Start? A Simple Instrument for Beginning Writing Program Assessment" *Journal of College Writing*, vol. 11, 2014, pp. 11–32.

Odom, Mary Lou. "Not Just for Writing Anymore: What WAC Can Teach Us About Reading to Learn." *Across the Disciplines*, vol. 10, no. 4, 2013, https://wac.colostate.edu/atd/reading/odom.cfm. Accessed 3 January 2022.

Pytlik, Betsy P. and Sarah Liggett, eds. *Preparing College Teachers of Writing: Histories, Theories, Programs, Practices*. Oxford UP, 2002.

Smit, David. "Curriculum Design for First-Year Writing Program." *The Allyn and Bacon Sourcebook for Writing Program Administrators*, edited by Irene Ward and William J. Carpenter, Longman, 2008, pp.185–206.

Sullivan, Patrick. "What Can We Learn about 'College-Level' Writing from Basic Writing Students? The Importance of Reading." *What is "College-Level" Writing? Volume 2*, edited by Patrick Sullivan, Howard Tinberg, and Sheridan Blau, NCTE, 2010, pp. 233–53.

Tate, Gary. "A Place for Literature in Freshman Composition." *College English*, vol. 55, no. 3, 1993, pp. 317–21.

Tremmel, Robert. "Seeking a Balanced Discipline: Writing Teacher Education in First-Year Composition and English Education." *English Education*, vol. 34, no. 1, 2001, pp. 6–30.

Yancey, Kathleen Blake. "The Professionalization of TA Development Programs: A Heuristic for Curriculum Design." Pytlik and Liggett, pp. 63–-74.

Liberty Kohn's interests are genre theory, rhetoric of social class, trust and emotion in public writing, and misinformation studies. He teaches courses in public writing, technical writing, and digital rhetoric at Winona State University. Kohn has directed the writing center, founded a WAC program, and chaired all-university Faculty Development at Winona State. His scholarship has appeared in the collections *Class in the Composition Classroom* (Utah State UP, 2017) and *Teaching Literature with Digital Technology: Assignments* (Bedford, 2016) as well as the *Journal of Technical Writing and Communication, Composition Forum, Journal of Working Class Studies, Journal of Interdisciplinary Humanities, Journal of Language Literacy and Education, Technoculture*, and more.

Designing DSP: UX and the Experience of Online Students

Kathleen Kryger and Catrina Mitchum

Abstract

Directed self-placement (DSP) is considered a student–centered and socially just tool for writing placement but rarely incorporates student–centered design methodologies. Though students are a vital stakeholder group in assessment and placement, they rarely take part in designing such systems. To begin addressing these contradictions, we implement user experience (UX) design methodologies to situate students-as-users of DSP systems, meaning that students are not simply consumers of DSP but are instead the locus of the design process, thus driving innovation and iteration. This article articulates a case study of implementing UX design methodologies to iterate on a writing program's current DSP system, focused particularly on better meeting online and transfer students' unique needs. By positioning students as co-designers and users of DSP, this article contributes to the expanding research on writing placement and the need for richly localized assessment designs.

The structuring of student pathways through placement and advising has lasting impacts on students' experiences in higher education, especially regarding their persistence and success at their institutions. Assessments have a powerful directionality component—the ability to usher students through particular academic pathways—and directed self-placement (DSP) is a perfect example. The stakes are high: initial placement outcomes can impact whether students go on to enroll in coursework (Adams, Gearhart, Miller, & Roberts, 2009; Messer, Gallagher, & Hart, 2022), whether they succeed in their classes (Inoue, 2009a; Klausman & Lynch, 2022), and whether they persist to degree (Valentine, Konstantopoulosm, & Goldrick-Rab, 2017). This research indicates that while placement is important for student success in first–year composition courses, it is also vital for students' overall progress to degree. Yet most of the research on DSP has focused on tools and outcomes rather than students' decision–making processes (Kenner, 2016; Saenkhum, 2016); such foci privilege students' experiences in the aggregate rather than the experiential or personal, often leaving administrators with more questions than answers. To mitigate some of these concerns, we iterated on one of our institution's DSP systems by seeking student feedback about their experiences—not just as a student in a course but also as a *user* of DSP.

DSP practices are, like all other writing assessment systems, sites of power, ideology, habituation. Placement practices are also rhetorical and function as part of a larger assessment ecology. Through the placement process, students engage with multiple rhetorical actors, often co-constructing their pathway through DSP alongside many others (family members or guardians, friends, academic advisors, placement advisors, orientation leaders, fellow students, previous educators, and more). Saenkhum (2016) recognizes how important these other participants are in influencing students' placement decisions, stating that, "students were able to exercise agency in their placement decision processes because of sufficient and necessary information they received from their academic advisors and from other students' past experiences" (p. 51). Wang (2020) argues that these complexities are at odds with the traditional premise of DSP and that the solution is to include negotiation as part of the process: "The 'twin fundamentals' of DSP, which are guidance and choice as Toth (2019) calls them, remain intact. Negotiation, the third fundamental, is what distinguishes the rhetorical model of DSP" (p. 53–54). This model aims to give students a chance to further develop their "emergent rhetorical agency" (p. 53). When viewed through a lens of social justice and technical and professional communication (TPC), we believe we can improve this negotiation aspect of DSP and better distribute the power of placement by including students in the process from the beginning of the design process. To shift the timing and distribution of power, we turn to user experience (UX) design models, in part because DSP constitutes a highly technical communicative endeavor and in part because TPC has a growing body of scholarship focused on equitable and participatory design systems.

DSP as Social Justice

While early DSP scholarship primarily investigated the purposes and content of DSP systems (Crusan, 2006, 2011; Royer & Gilles, 1998, 2003, 2012; Toth & Aull, 2014), recent scholarship is more interested in the social and academic consequences of DSP's implementation, particularly regarding equity for diverse populations and two-year colleges (Nastal, Poe, & Toth, 2022). For instance, Inoue's (2009b) racial validity framework focuses on disaggregating local assessment data to reveal potential racial formations and their comparative outcomes. Methodologies of disparate impact analysis take up this work with a particular focus on legally protected populations (see Poe, Elliot, Cogan, & Nurudeen, 2014). Toth

(2018) usefully summarizes these and other attempts as "validation for social justice" (p. 145), suggesting that more research is needed to continue substantiating DSP's local impacts on student equity. When analyzing DSP's potential to serve two-year college populations, Toth (2018) writes, "DSP's ability to achieve that promise [of social justice] is contingent on processes designed with a critical awareness of ideologies that reproduce social inequalities. . . . This labor must be undertaken carefully, critically, and continuously" (p. 151). When situated within the "Fourth Wave" of writing assessment scholarship (Behm & Miller, 2012), student self-placement must be understood as a social justice endeavor, especially because placement has serious implications for student enrollment, retention, and success (Klausman & Lynch, 2022; Toth, 2019; VanOra, 2019). Despite being the population most directly impacted, undergraduate students are rarely included in the design process of writing placements.

DSP as Technical Communication

DSP must also be understood as a complex set of technical communication acts. Technical communication can be summarized in four concepts: technical communication (1) "exists to accomplish something"; (2) "is a form of social action"; (3) "seeks to make tacit knowledge explicit"; and (4) relates to technology, with a broad conception of "technology" that encompasses "knowledge, actions, and tools" (Durack, 1997, p. 257–258). By these and other definitions, DSP is technical communication: it exists to help students choose a college composition course/sequence; this requirement of a decision, the decision–making process, and its implications are all certainly social action; it seeks to make first-year writing course/sequence knowledge explicit; and it is often mediated through technology in several ways. Additionally, DSP can be further understood as intercultural technical communication, given that it must function for increasingly diverse student populations (across various educational, sociopolitical, transnational, legal, and linguistic contexts). Because DSP systems seek to make our field's specialized knowledge usable to incoming students and other stakeholders, we argue that TPC methodologies are relevant to their design, implementation, and iteration—meaning that they can (and should) be improved by UX research.

Agboka's (2013, 2014) participatory localization framework suggests that developers (in this case, administrators and staff) work alongside the users (incoming students, including transfer and non-traditional students) when designing their tool/technology (writing placement systems, particularly DSP) rather than having the users passively consume the final product.

Challenging such practices as they relate to developing tools across international contexts, Agboka (2013) argues that "technical communication may participate in the colonial exploitation and objectification of users in cultural sites, especially those in disempowered, unenfranchised cultural sites, if localization practices are not reconceptualized to place users at par with the developer in the design process" (p. 31). As currently conceived, placement is not facilitated by student-centered technologies; instead, placement assessment systems are technical products designed with the intent of imposition. That is, administrators and staff design systems and impose them on students rather than inviting students to design alongside us, thus removing a crucial opportunity to lower power imbalances and bolster student agency. Below, we articulate a tangible first step toward positioning students as equals in the DSP design process.

Purposes of the Research

To investigate students' experiences with our online campus DSP tool, we designed a UX project that would specifically invite student feedback on our iteration process.[1] DSP systems (in this article, we sometimes use the phrase "DSP system[s]" because DSP often involves far more than a single tool) benefit from the methodologies of participatory localization and UX design for not only iterating tools but also prioritizing students' experiences and needs. While the overall goals of DSP have aligned well with writing pedagogy for decades, and while DSP is recognized as a potentially equitable means of student placement, little research has been done on placement of online or transfer students (Gere et al., 2017; Toth, 2018; Toth, 2019), and no research has yet framed DSP as technical communication.

Part of equity and effectiveness in TPC is the inclusion and understanding of all user groups. Online and transfer students are often overlooked in the placement and advising systems at major universities where first-year students represent the bulk of enrollments, and transfer students tend to be a more diverse pool of students than the typical incoming cohorts of "true" freshmen (Chamely-Wiik et al., 2021; Rosenberg, 2016). Most transfer students have part- or full-time jobs (though that is becoming more common for all college students, not just transfer or returning students); transfer students are more likely to be returning students; transfer students are often caretakers or providers of income for their families (Chamely-Wiik et al., 2021). According to research in retention studies and elsewhere, students who transfer from one institution to another are more likely to get stuck, time out, or lose their place in their academic journeys (Blekic, Carpenter, & Cao, 2020; Boston, Ice, & Burgess, 2012; Mamiseishvili & Deggs, 2013).

Of the students who completed our DSP tool in 2021, 76.5% were transfer or re-admit students, and our DSP questionnaire had very few questions addressing the unique needs of that part of our community. On the whole, online and transfer students represent a cohort with needs that differ from traditional cohorts of first-year freshmen, and through our UX case study, we were able to address some of those needs at our local institution.

In this article, we demonstrate how our UX project improved an existing DSP system by unearthing student concerns, in concrete ways, and involving students in the questionnaire revision process. The goal of this article is two-fold:

1. To supplement ongoing placement research that demonstrates the need for richly localized DSP systems, especially for under-supported populations (such as online, transfer, and multilingual students).
2. To highlight the need for and importance of incorporating TPC methodologies (such as UX design and/or participatory localization) in service of further localizing DSP systems.

By sharing our work on this case study, we hope to provide strategies for programs interested in developing a DSP system, as well as ideas for iterative improvement for already established systems. Without student input, we are only ever seeing a small part of the puzzle.

INSTITUTIONAL CONTEXT

Positionalities

This research was conducted at the University of Arizona, a large, public, land-grant, Research 1 university in the southwestern United States. This land was seized from Indigenous Peoples and allocated to land-grant universities in accordance with the Morrill Act, which was signed into law by President Lincoln in 1862 (Ahtone, 2020; Lee & Ahtone, 2020; Lee et al., 2020). As a land-grant university, the university benefits from the possession of the traditional lands of the Tohono O'odham Nation, whose predecessors include the Hohokam and the O'odham, as well as the Pascua Yaqui Peoples. Over the centuries, these communities have been continuously impacted by various land cessions. It is vital that we as scholars and teachers understand the histories of our institutions and the legacies of harm that sustain them (Vowel, 2016).

The authors are both White cisgender women born in the United States, with English as their first language, and they exist in proximity to a great deal of sociopolitical privilege. Kathleen is neurodivergent, queer, and chronically ill, and was, at the time of research and writing, a graduate candidate at the University of Arizona. Her positionality as a neurodivergent graduate administrator influenced the scholarship used to argue for DSP as a site of social justice, with her interests particularly focusing on accessibility and disability justice in writing assessment. Catrina has a chronic illness that decides when it wants to impact her cognitive functioning, is a military spouse, and was a distance student herself. At the time of this study, she was also the Interim Director of Online Writing. These positionalities influenced her decision to pursue teaching and research in online spaces and so influenced the portion of the data from the larger study that this piece focuses on.

Start of DSP in our Writing Program

Like many others, our university was impacted by changes to College Board's SAT scoring procedures in 2016. While the writing program had been considering DSP and other multiple measures placement methods well before then, the shift away from dependence on standardized exam scores for placement allowed us to capitalize on a kairotic moment and try something new. We were already in the process of shifting placement systems for our international student populations, but after 2016, we committed to shifting to DSP for all incoming domestic students (both first-year and transfer). By 2018, we had built and launched our first DSP system, which was dubbed the Foundations Writing Evaluation (FWE).

Our DSP (FWE) System

Our DSP system, the FWE, now includes several features: (1) an intricate Qualtrics online survey tool; (2) year-round asynchronous email advising; (3) synchronous orientation session advising; and (4) a "Handy Guide to Foundations Writing" webpage. We currently have discrete versions of this Qualtrics tool for a few different student populations: international students, main campus students, global students (international online campus), and online campus students. The Qualtrics tool is the central feature of our DSP system, and it relies on an internal web service that reads secure student information (such as transcripts) and can, as students complete the FWE, filter relevant information regarding their course/sequence options. Additionally, students can report pending dual enrollment/transfer credits as well as relevant exam scores, select a course placement, and request additional one-on-one support from placement advisors. Most of the FWEs include a course recommendation, one or two small writing tasks, and a link to the "Handy Guide." The Qualtrics tool also implements a self-assessment questionnaire that inquires into students' histories with various literacy tasks and classroom learning preferences. Though, in this article, we focus primarily on the questionnaire aspect of our tool, we provide these details to contextualize our local DSP system and to acknowledge the complexities of placement administration labor.

Creation of oFWE

In the fall semester of 2020, the online campus student success team administrators requested a FWE specific to our online student population. This tool was created, but it was also provisionally stripped of the main–campus questionnaire items because our online students did not have all the same course/sequence options available to them. As online course options expanded, however, it became clear that the online-campus FWE (oFWE) needed to be revised with questionnaire items specific to online–campus population needs.

Why Now?

In 2017, the upper administration of our online campus requested a pilot of a four-credit equivalent course in Foundations Writing. This request was based on the writing program's success with ENGL101A (a four-credit course that offers students an hour of writing studio time). Since the request, the online model for the last four years has been to offer our traditional three-credit courses (101/102) with a one-credit co-curricular (197B) writing workshop. Aside from the student population and the goals of the extra credit hour, a significant difference between 101A and 101/102 with 197B is placement. Our main-campus students can self-place into 101A using the main-campus FWE. Our online campus students, however, were enrolled in 197B by the writing program based on one criterion: whether it was their first writing course at the institution. This one-credit course was free to these students, and they were manually enrolled by staff in our writing program. Part of the reason for both using this metric and for comping the credit hour is that online students pay per credit hour as opposed to per semester, meaning that our online students are often less willing to enroll in a four-credit course than a main-campus student. For the pilot, the online campus covered the cost of the extra credit hour for students.

The pilot for 197B was considered a success (as measured by the improvement in student grades over time since 2017). The online campus thus elected to end the pilot, and the writing program now offers an official four-credit course to replace the 197B co-curricular model we were using.

This means that students must now pay for that extra credit hour and have the opportunity to self-place into either the three- or four-credit course.

This exigence was an opportunity to build a DSP questionnaire in ways we didn't in 2018: with the student perspective. We created our UX project with the goals of not just utilizing student feedback to iterate on our DSP but also of engaging students in every phase of the study, of positioning them as active contributors rather than passive consumers of our DSP, and of centering their experiences in ways that incorporate goals of social justice (Agboka, 2013; Jones, 2016). To ensure our oFWE provides fair and valid guidance in assessing online students' needs, we conducted focus groups of students who completed the one-credit co-curricular. Using the focus group data, we crafted new oFWE questionnaire items, which were then further studied with usability testing. Finally, the larger UX study includes a follow-up survey at the end of the semester to determine whether students felt they were placed appropriately. Below, we provide more details about our methods, results, and implementations.

Methods

Models of UX design and research are driven by the goal of developing iterative, collaborative, and user-focused designs, and there is no commonly accepted rigid definition of UX design. Instead, UX design blends methodologies from various disciplines, such as human computer interaction, information architecture, computer science, and user interface design (see Gläser, Jaritz, & Sackl, 2013 for a visual representation), and it often incorporates principles of accessibility and usability. UX also emphasizes the importance of iterative design and user input before launching as well as a design process that is adaptive and ongoing (Chow & Sajonas, 2020). UX design thus views users (broadly construed) as the central unit of the ecology rather than as a group that has designs done to them (Agboka, 2013; Robinson, Lanius, & Weber, 2017). This shift in positionality is important for DSP because it allows students to be the locus of the design rather than institutional data. Though we must, of course, take into consideration things such as number of course sections, distribution of placements, grades, and retention, localized student needs ought to be the center of the DSP's design. To be clear, UX research is different from a simple usability test because of that shift to ongoing experiences and the importance of user input before, during, and after a design (Babich, 2020). Usability testing, which focuses on aspects like user interface and visual design, falls under the broader UX design umbrella. For our purposes in this phase of the study, we adapted UX principles to focus on human-centered participatory design, another aspect of the UX umbrella.

Though our program's larger UX study included all our FWE tools, in this article, we focus particularly on the oFWE, which serves our online campus students. As mentioned above, because there was a unique opportunity to garner student input before crafting questions, the case study on the oFWE consisted of three phases: (1) small focus groups with participants from the target user population, that is, students who were placed into the one-credit co-curricular the previous year; (2) usability tests where students evaluate the new questionnaire items; and (3) a validity survey to determine if students felt their placement was a good fit. During the focus group phase, students discussed their experiences with 197B and the placement system, and then they brainstormed questions for future students taking 197B. We then took the rich descriptions of student experiences to craft oFWE questionnaire items. In this piece, we will share the newly developed questionnaire items and select focus group data. The results of these focus groups were used to craft new questions for the oFWE, and they were also used to improve the curriculum as the co-curricular transitioned from a parallel course to an interwoven credit. The new oFWE was then part of a usability test, designed as a think-aloud protocol, to glimpse how students are processing the newly implemented oFWE questionnaire items.

For the focus groups, we solicited participation from students who were enrolled in 197B in the academic year 2020–2021. The goal was to conduct three focus groups of five students (one hour each), and students were offered $20 Amazon gift cards for their participation. We conducted these focus groups in summer 2021, and we had five participants across two focus group sessions, which were conducted by Kathleen and used a specific set of seven questions as a guide (see the appendix). The interviewer facilitated conversations centering on students' experiences with the following topics: reactions to their placement in 197B, descriptions in their own words of 197B, the usefulness of 197B, advice to future students taking the course, and changes they would make. In each session, follow-up questions were asked for clarification.

After the focus group transcripts were validated against the recordings and de-identified, the responses were analyzed using in-vivo coding for a first round and values coding in a second round (Saldaña, 2016), with two coders attending norming sessions to ensure that they were applying codes in similar ways. The codes were then grouped into the following themes: (1) placement issues, (2) curriculum, (3) value, and (4) DSP questions.

Results and Discussion

For the purposes of this article, we share selected data related to the themes of placement issues and DSP questions. While we cannot fully address the curricular concerns that arose during our case study, they were taken into consideration as the writing program shifted to the official four-credit course option. We had only five students participate in the focus groups, so we consider this research to be a case study specific to our context. Of those five students, four self-identified as transfer students during the focus groups. This focus group population is key to understanding some of the codes that showed up. The placement issues theme was divided into two areas: (1) placement issues related to the one-credit co-curricular course (ENGL197B) and (2) placement issues related to Foundations Writing in general. The placement issues around 197B (see table 1) were not surprising, as there was never a good enrollment process established during the co-curricular course's pilot.

Table 1
97B Placement Issues Sample Responses

Theme	Code	Samples
197B Placement Issues	Add-on/last-minute placement	"now they add this other class"
		"I didn't know I was enrolled in the course"
	Affective response to placement	"blindsided"
		"kinda shocked"
	Time concerns related to the last-minute placement	"I had to even put some of the time in to do them"
		"I had to be very careful with the timing, and now they add this other class"
	Age/experience felt like misplacement	"helpful towards first years who don't have much experience in English composition"
		"And I think probably because I'm older and I've been working for a long time"

This data confirms that the last-minute non-self-placement for 197B resulted in student stress regarding having the time to complete the course. Students were concerned about the added work of 197B, in addition to the confusion created by the placement process and criteria.

What was unexpected were the other placement concerns students had, which were largely associated with the students who self-identified as transfer students (see table 2). We know transfer students are more likely to drop out due to credit transfer and articulation issues (Blekic, Carpenter, & Cao, 2020; Boston, Ice, & Burgess, 2012). Providing space for this particular group to articulate their concerns provided us with concrete considerations for improving our placement processes for this group's unique needs. These affordances would not have been possible without centering student voices through the participatory methods described above.

Table 2
Placement Issues Not Related to Co-Curricular Placement

Theme	Code	Samples
Non-197B Placement Issues	Course not available	"placed in an honors class, but the honors class wasn't offered online"
	Being a senior	"I'm currently a junior-almost senior-level student in upper courses being told to go back and pretend to be a freshman; I'm a senior, and I've been submitting very, very intense writing assignments with no issue. So having to go back . . ."
	Previous similar courses/work that didn't transfer	"my credits had transferred in a very strange way"
		"I took a CLEP test that existed back then (apparently doesn't exist anymore)"
		"writing is a huge part of my job"

The array of placement issues unrelated to enrollment in 197B was quite specific to transfer students. While these topics weren't why we set out to do this study (our initial interest was online students more broadly), they emphasize the ongoing need to ensure that our DSP questionnaires and supporting materials consider how our writing program serves this student population. The majority of our focus group participants were advanced in their academic (and professional) careers, and it's possible that at least one student, seen in row two of table 2, was a senior who elected to not take their first-year writing in their first year. This is not an uncommon phenomenon in online campuses where students aren't given auto-enrollments.

In our focus groups, students also articulated the value of 197B for future students and described the students who would likely most benefit from the course. In table 3, we share the codes for those themes that are relevant to oFWE questionnaire design. Focus group participants felt that students might benefit from and/or want to be enrolled in the official four-credit course for two main reasons: (1) additional support through regularly scheduled one-on-one conferences with the instructor, and (2) the sustained support provided for completing the writing assignments and projects in the "core" composition class.

From table 3, we crafted three items for the oFWE questionnaire. We also selected ten of the current nineteen items of the main-campus FWE self-assessment, specifically focusing on the items related to ENGL101A, our main-campus four-credit studio course. The three questions generated from the focus group data are listed as statements with Likert-style responses. The three oFWE questionnaire items are:

1. I feel comfortable reaching out to my instructors for help.
2. I am able to successfully complete writing assignments without assistance from my instructor.
3. I feel confident in my writing.

Each item includes the following options that are given the "score" listed next to them:

- Not really (1)
- Kind of (2)
- Mostly (3)
- Absolutely (3)

Table 3

Value of the One-Credit Co-Curricular Course

Theme	Code	Sample
197B Value	*Relationship with and access to instructor*	"value for 197B would definitely be the access to the instructor" "I just felt more comfortable asking him questions in the future because we built a bit of a rapport" [without 197B] "It may have been more difficult for me to approach a professor, ask questions, get to the heart of an issue that I might be having"
	Assignment/ course design	"a resource for those who may not or who would like extra" "the assignments that directly were aimed at or applicable to assignments in the class that you were already doing" "helpful in that some of the curriculum... corresponded to the curriculum we were doing in the course"
	For "others"	"would've been beneficial for those students that this is their first course online or maybe they're returning to school after a long time" "[struggle] with writing in general"
Questions for DSP	*Asking for help*	"ask them if they're the type of students that don't reach out for help, maybe they should be put into 197B because it'll be a more convenient way for them to get help"
	Writing confidence/ experience	"writing is a huge part of my job, so like working at a hospital with doctors, you can't just send an email that looks like a text message. It has to be pretty formal, all the time. So, I mean, finding out what they do as part of their job, for writing."

The DSP self-assessment questionnaire begins with eight questions that focus on student comfort levels with their writing experience, then moves into five questions focused on how much support students feel they need in specific elements of learning how to write in an online class. These items provide space for students to think more holistically about their learning process, rather than limiting their self-assessment to only writing and reading skills and tasks. Involving student stakeholders and honoring their wisdom and experiences should always inform the "guidance" aspect of DSP. This study has helped us become more pointed and more selective in our questions for specific user populations, and we hope to learn more as we continue including students in the iteration of our DSP system.

Usability Study Results

The second stage of our three-part UX case study consisted of a usability test of the new questionnaire items developed for the oFWE (as opposed to the tool itself, which had already undergone separate usability testing by a group of student users, and then substantive revisions, in early 2020). We used a think–aloud protocol, asking students to read and respond aloud to the oFWE questionnaire items and then consider whether they felt their placement was accurate based on their assigned scenario. The three scenarios crafted for this usability test included having a choice between the three- and four-credit course for both semesters, as well as a choice between the transfer portfolio and the transfer-student course.

Our UX projects, including this case study, were continually constrained by the ongoing pandemic and the unique time constraints of online students, resulting in small sample sizes. Despite offering $50 gift cards for participating, only three students agreed to participate. These students were different from those in the focus groups. Of the three usability test responses, one was unusable because the student muted the audio when they entered the Zoom room. The other two tests were coded for hesitancy and confidence in answering each question.

Student 3, who completed scenario three, was confident in answering twelve out of the thirteen questions. This student read the questions and potential responses out loud and then selected their responses immediately for those twelve questions. The final question came with some "it depends" hedging about being "open to suggestions" and resulted in the student selecting a response indicating they needed little to no assistance. These hesitations were interpreted as the student reflecting on their experiences and fitting those experiences into the question parameters as opposed to the question being difficult to answer.

Student 2, who completed scenario two, was confident in answering six of the thirteen questions. This student talked through their reasoning for how they were responding to every question where the answer was not "absolutely." That reasoning centered around their experiences, their comfort level, and their ideas of how contextual factors could impact their behavior. This hesitancy was also interpreted as reflecting on their experience to answer the question. However, this particular student used the phrase "it depends" in response to three questions that asked about how much guidance or assistance from "peers and instructor" was needed. For this student, where the assistance came from made a difference.

Both students also answered the usability follow-up questions and indicated the following: (1) the course recommendation provided by the oFWE questionnaire results would be a good fit based on how they answered the questions; (2) the questionnaire items helped develop their understanding of what both the three- and four-credit options would offer them personally; and (3) the questions were "straightforward and easy to answer."

The students didn't hesitate to answer the three questions created from the focus group data. The results of this usability test were used to adjust the phrasing in the assistance questions from "and" to "and/or," thus providing space for students to consider assistance and guidance from either party because the four-credit hour course will provide extra assistance and guidance from both peers and their instructor. Otherwise, the results indicated that the 197B focus-group questions were useful in making course recommendations.

The third and final step of our UX case study is a single-question survey asking students if the class they're currently enrolled in is a good fit for them. This step has been on hold since 2022, waiting for the four-credit course to be officially added to the course catalog.

Limitations

In addition to the timing of the study during the pandemic and the low participation, we want to acknowledge that diving deeper into students' intersecting identities is not something we were able to consider. Catrina was the Interim Director of the Online Writing Program at the time, and Kathleen was the Assistant Director of Placement and Assessment, and we both were careful about protecting student identities, and not asking too much of our staff during a very stressful and overwhelming time. Future iterations should include this information.

Conclusion

DSP systems are created with students' best interests at heart, but as Inoue (2009b) and others have noted, assessment technologies have latent structures of power and ideology, many of which are harmful to students. Our preliminary case study research demonstrates the potential of UX for placement: UX provides structures of both participatory localization and student-focused methodologies. While our study includes a DSP system already designed and in use, one built by staff members and graduate students researching current best practices in placement, we believe undergraduate students ought to be involved with the DSP design process from the very beginning. They are the central user group of placement systems, and their academic careers (and their lives/livelihoods) are heavily impacted by these systems.

While this project is just the beginning of our three-stage UX study on our oFWE, the resulting data, as well as the unexpected inclusion of transfer student perspectives, suggests that UX methodologies are one way to ensure we're serving all our diverse student populations. Because placement is a hugely complex process for most American colleges and universities, rife with intricacies of dual enrollment, exam scores, transfer credits, national/state/local policies, and articulation agreements, we understand the importance of valuing administrator expertise. But we also know that students are at the core of our work, and the more we can work alongside them rather than for them, the more we can distribute power in meaningful ways.

Once DSP has been situated as both a site of social justice and technical communication, we can see how Agboka's (2013, 2014) concerns about disenfranchising the user (if users passively consume the final product) come to fruition—and how a DSP system can unintentionally function in direct opposition to its purpose. By shifting our understanding of DSP to include UX aspects of design and implementation, and therefore including students-as-users in the (re)design process, writing program administrators can ensure more localized, effective, and equitable DSP design and results. Small, contextualized changes can sometimes be the driving force of an iterative and locally responsive DSP system.

Appendix

Focus Group Questions

1. What was your first reaction to being placed in 197B? Why?
2. If you could describe the 197B course in 1–2 sentences (elevator pitch), what would it be?
3. If you felt the experience was useful, why is that? What benefit did 197B offer you during the course?
4. How do you feel your 197B experience has helped you in other courses? In what ways did it help?
5. If you were to give a future 197B student advice, what would it be?
6. If we define a *workshop* as a space for reviewing and revising and define a *studio* as a space where you get extra help with your work and your writing, do you feel that 197B was a workshop or a studio?
7. If you had a magic wand or a time machine, what would you have changed about your 197B experience?

Note

1. IRB Protocol Number: 2106926122

References

Adams, Peter D., Gearhart, Sarah, Miller, Robert, & Roberts, Anne. (2009). The accelerated learning program: Throwing open the gates. *Journal of Basic Writing, 28*(2), 50–69. https://doi.org/10.37514/JBW-J.2009.28.2.04

Agboka, Godwin Y. (2013). Participatory localization: A social justice approach to navigating unenfranchised/disenfranchised cultural sites. *Technical Communication Quarterly, 22*(1), 28–49. https://doi.org/10.1080/10572252.2013.730966

Agboka, Godwin Y. (2014). Decolonial methodologies: Social justice perspectives in intercultural technical communication research. *Journal of Technical Writing and Communication, 44*(3), 297–327. https://doi.org/10.2190/TW.44.3.e

Ahtone, Tristan. (2020, March 30). Lost and found: The story of land-grant universities. *High Country News*. https://www.hcn.org/issues/52.4/editors-note-lost-and-found-the-story-of-land-grant-universities

Babich, Nicholas. (2020, November 24). What you should know about user experience design. XD Ideas, Adobe. https://xd.adobe.com/ideas/career-tips/what-is-ux-design/

Behm, Nicholas, & Miller, Keith D. (2012). Challenging the frameworks of colorblind racism: Why we need a fourth wave of writing assessment scholarship. In Asao B. Inoue & Maya Poe (Eds.), *Race and writing assessment* (pp. 127–140). Peter Lang Publishing.

Blekic, Mirela, Carpenter, Rowanna, & Cao, Yi. (2020). Continuing and transfer students: Exploring retention and second-year success. *Journal of College Student Retention: Research, Theory and Practice, 22*(1), 71–98. https://doi.org/10.1177/1521025117726048

Boston, Wallace, Ice, Phil, & Burgess, Melissa. (2012). Assessing student retention in online learning environments: A longitudinal study. *Online Journal of Distance Learning Administration, 15*(2).

Chamely-Wiik, Donna, Frazier, Evelyn, Meeroff, Daniel, Merritt, Jordan, Johnson, Jodiene, Kwochka, William R., Morrison-Shetlar, Alison I., Aldarondo-Jeffries, Michael, & Schneider, Kimberly R. (2021). Undergraduate research communities for transfer students: A retention model based on factors that most influence student success. *Journal of the Scholarship of Teaching and Learning, 21*(1), 193–224. https://doi.org/10.14434/josotl.v21i1.30273

Chow, L., & Sajonas, Sandra. (2020). From UX study to UX service: Using people-centered research methods to improve the public library experience. *Public Library Quarterly, 39*(6), 493–509.

Crusan, Deborah. (2006). The politics of implementing online directed self-placement for second language writers. In Paul Kei Matsuda, Christina Ortmeier-

Hooper, & Xizoye You (Eds.), *The politics of second language writing: In search of the promised land* (pp. 205–221). Parlor Press.

Crusan, Deborah. (2011). The promise of directed self-placement for second language writers. *TESOL Quarterly, 45*(4), 774–780.

Durack, Katherine T. (1997). Gender, technology, and the history of technical communication. *Technical Communication Quarterly, 6*(3), 249–260.

Gere, Anne R., Hutton, Lizzie, Keating, Benjamin, Knutson, Anna V., Silver, Naomi, & Toth, Christie. (2017). Mutual adjustments: Learning from and responding to transfer student writers. *College English, 79*(4), 333–357.

Gläser, Thomas, Jaritz, Markus, & Sackl, Philipp. (2013, April 22). *Mapping the disciplines of user experience design*. Envis precisely, GitHub. https://github.com/envisprecisely/disciplines-of-ux

Inoue, Asao B. (2009a). Self-assessment as programmatic center: The first-year writing program and its assessment at California State University, Fresno. *Composition Forum, 20.*

Inoue, Asao B. (2009b). The technology of writing assessment and racial validity. In C. Schreiner (Ed.), *Handbook of research on assessment technologies, methods, and applications in higher education* (pp. 97–120). Information Science Reference.

Jones, Natasha N. (2016). The technical communicator as advocate: Integrating a social justice approach in technical communication. *Journal of Technical Writing and Communication, 46*(3), 342–362. https://doi.org/10.1177/0047281616639472

Kenner, Kylie. (2016). Student rationale for self-placement into first-year composition: Decision making and directed self-placement. *Teaching English in the Two-Year College, 43*(3), 274–289. https://library.ncte.org/journals/TETYC/issues/v43-3/28377

Klausman, Jeffrey, & Lynch, Signee. (2022). From ACCUPLACER to information self-placement at Whatcom Community College: Equitable placement as an evolving practice. In Jessica Nastal, Maya Poe, & Christie Toth (Eds.), *Writing placement in two-year colleges: The pursuit of equity in postsecondary education* (pp. 59–83). The WAC Clearinghouse; University Press of Colorado. https://doi.org/10.37514/PRA-B.2022.1565

Lee, Robert, & Ahtone, Tristan. (2020, May 19). How they did it: Exposing how U.S. universities profited from Indigenous land. *Global Investigative Journalism Network*. https://pulitzercenter.org/stories/how-they-did-it-exposing-how-us-universities-profited-indigenous-land

Lee, Robert, Ahtone, Tristan, Pearce, Margaret, Goodluck, Kalen, McGhee, Geoff, Leff, Cody, Lanpher, Katherine, & Salinas, Taryn. (2020, March 30). Land-grab universities. *High Country News*. https://www.landgrabu.org/

Mamiseishvili, Ketevan, & Deggs, David M. (2013). Factors affecting persistence and transfer of low-income students at public two-year institutions. *Journal of College Student Retention: Research, Theory and Practice, 15*(3), 409–432. doi:10.2190/CS.15.3.f

Messer, Kris, Gallagher, Jamey, & Hart, Elizabeth. (2022). A path to equity, agency, and access: Self-directed placement at the Community College of Baltimore County. In Jessica Nastal, Maya Poe, & Christie Toth (Eds.), *Writing placement in two-year colleges: The pursuit of equity in postsecondary education* (pp. 85–105). The WAC Clearinghouse; University Press of Colorado. https://doi.org/10.37514/PRA-B.2022.1565.2.03

Nastal, Jessica, Poe, Mya, & Toth, Christie. (Eds.). (2022). *Writing placement in two-year colleges: The pursuit of equity in postsecondary education*. The WAC Clearinghouse; University Press of Colorado. https://doi.org/10.37514/PRA-B.2022.1565

Poe, Mya, Elliot, Norbert, Cogan, John A., Jr., & Nurudeen, Tito G., Jr. (2014). The legal and the local: Using disparate impact analysis to understand the consequences of writing assessment. *College Composition and Communication*, 65(4), 588–611.

Robinson, Joy, Lanius, Candice, & Weber, Ryan. (2017). The past, present, and future of UX research. *Communication Design Quarterly*, 5(3), 10–23. https://doi.org/10.1145/3188173.3188175

Rosenberg, Michael J. (2016). Understanding the adult transfer student—Support, concerns, and transfer student capital. *Community College Journal of Research and Practice*, 40(12), 1058–1073. https://doi.org/10.1080/10668926.2016.1216907

Royer, Daniel, & Gilles, Roger. (1998). Directed self-placement: An attitude of orientation. *College Composition and Communication*, 50(1), 54–70.

Royer, Daniel J., & Gilles, Roger. (Eds.) (2003). *Directed self-placement: Principles and practices*. Hampton Press, Inc.

Royer, Daniel J., & Gilles, Roger. (2012). The private and the public in directed self-placement. In N. Elliot & L. Perelman (Eds.), *Writing assessment in the 21st century: Essays in honor of Edward White* (pp. 363–369). Hampton Press, Inc.

Saldaña, Johnny. (2016). *The coding manual for qualitative researchers*. (3rd ed.). SAGE Publications.

Saenkhum, Tanita. (2016). *Decisions, agency, and advising: Key issues in the placement of multilingual writers into first-year composition courses*. Utah State University Press.

Toth, Christie. (2018). Chapter 4. Directed self-placement at "Democracy's Open Door": Writing placement and social justice in community colleges. In M. Poe, A. B. Inoue, & N. Elliot (Eds.), *Writing assessment, social justice, and the advancement of opportunity* (pp. 137–170). The WAC Clearinghouse; University Press of Colorado. https://doi.org/10.37514/PER-B.2018.0155.2.04

Toth, Christie. (2019). Directed self-placement at two-year colleges: A kairotic moment. *Journal of Writing Assessment*. 12(1). https://escholarship.org/uc/item/6g81k736

Toth, Christie, & Aull, Laura. (2014). Directed self-placement questionnaire design: Practices, problems, possibilities. *Assessing Writing*, 20, 1–18. https://dx.doi.org/10.1016/j.asw.2013.11.006

Valentine, Jeffrey. C., Konstantopoulos, Spyros., & Goldrick-Rab, Sara. (2017). What happens to students placed into developmental education? A meta-analysis of regression discontinuity studies. *Review of Educational Research, 87*(4), 806–833. https://doi.org/10.3102/0034654317709237

VanOra, Jason. (2019). "It's Like One Step for Me to Go Forward": A longitudinal study of community college students' perceptions on the value of developmental education. *Community College Enterprise, 25*(1), 59–76.

Vowel, Chelsea. (2016, September 23). *Beyond territorial acknowledgments*. âpihtawikosisân. https://apihtawikosisan.com/2016/09/beyond-territorial-acknowledgments/

Wang, Zhaozhe. (2020). Toward a rhetorical model of directed self-placement. *WPA: Writing Program Administration, 44*(1), 45–67.

Kathleen Kryger recently concluded her doctoral degree at the University of Arizona. She was the Writing Instruction Specialist for the University of Arizona's University Center for Assessment, Teaching, and Technology (UCATT), where she led several multidisciplinary teacher learning communities on alternative forms of classroom assessment. While this research was conducted, she worked as the writing program's Graduate Assistant Director of Placement and Assessment. She has been doing and teaching technical writing since 2013. Her scholarship continues to explore the intersections of writing assessment, user experience (UX), and disability justice. Her work can be found in the *Journal of Writing Assessment*.

Catrina Mitchum is adjuncting as it was intended as associate professor at University of Maryland Global Campus. She is co-author of *Teaching Literacy Online*. She has been designing and teaching online courses since 2009 and has been awarded various teaching awards. She has taught first-year writing, professional and technical writing, and introduction to research, entirely online. She is driven to create access for students. She was awarded, with other scholars, the CCCC Research Initiative Grant in 2018 and a Digital Learning Tech Seed Grant in 2021, and in 2021–2022, she was an Inclusive Leadership Fellow.

Building Effective Arguments about Writing Class Size and Workload

Todd Ruecker and Galen Gorelangton

Abstract

Our field has long recognized the value of keeping writing classes small; however, the reality in most institutions does not match these values and WPAs often struggle to successfully advocate around class size and workload. With this struggle in mind, we conducted semi-structured interviews with twenty WPAs from a variety of institution types about their experiences advocating for their programs around class size and workload. Using a Burkean framework, we explore the challenges humanist-oriented WPAs faced while advocating with neoliberal-oriented administrators as well as a variety of rhetorical strategies they harnessed to make progress, such as identifying and building on administrative priorities and partnering with other departments and units.

Class size has long been a point of contention between writing teachers, WPAs, and upper administration. Members of CCCC, CWPA, and other writing organizations have long recognized the value of keeping writing classes small, a value reflected in statements such as the *CCCC Principles for the Postsecondary Teaching of Writing* statement. With larger classes and higher teaching loads the norm in many places, many have found that such statements have little sway with upper administrators looking to writing programs to cut costs. As Cassandra Phillips and Greg Ahrenhoerster note, "We knew, however, that there was little hope of meeting these recommendations" in part because they were already well above those thresholds and because the proposed budget cuts were "dramatic" (10). Nonetheless, as Alice Horning pointed out in 2007, there is not "a solid empirical study to demonstrate, once and for all, that smaller classes help students become more effective writers in college" (11). As we will discuss in more detail below, Horning's point is still very much a reality today—whereas there have been a variety of studies on the impact of class size on students and faculty in a variety of fields, there is still not definitive evidence that smaller class sizes boost student success as defined by passing and graduation rates, metrics that administrators often most care about.

The present study does not provide that definitive answer. As we will discuss, a variety of contextual nuances (e.g., institution type, leadership, community values) can make that answer largely elusive. Moreover, it is evident that administrators are not always swayed by the results of meticulous research. They are often driven more by their own interests, policy goals set at the state level, or budgetary constraints. With these limitations in mind, we set to build on existing work about WPA advocacy to investigate the ways that WPAs have successfully and unsuccessfully advocated for smaller class sizes and how their work has been shaped by various contextual factors. Ultimately, we believe that by learning how our colleagues from around the country have made the case for smaller class sizes, WPAs can more effectively learn to frame our arguments in ways that administrators find convincing (Adler-Kassner, *Activist*).

Research on Class Size

There have been a variety of smaller studies as well as meta-analyses on the impact of class size on teaching and learning in K-12 and higher education contexts over the years—some focused explicitly on writing classes while other work focused more broadly on general education programs or institutions as a whole. These studies have coalesced around a few different areas: impact on grades and retention rates (Ake-Little, von der Embse, and Dawson; Diette and Raghav; Glau; Kokkelenberg, Dillon, and Christy), impact on student satisfaction (Cuseo; Bedard and Kuhn; Queen), and impact on pedagogical choices (e.g., Lee; Roberts-Miller, "Class Size"; "Class Size Another"). Whereas this research hasn't produced consistent and compelling evidence that smaller classes lead to greater student retention, the findings are consistent that students prefer smaller classes.

One finding is clear for writing instructors, however—the larger the class, the less time that teachers have giving students the individualized feedback that is so central to our courses. Richard Haswell calculated that a teacher spending adequate time giving feedback on student work would hit overtime hours if teaching only three writing classes a semester. Horning points to limited evidence that revision and feedback are more likely to happen in smaller classes, explaining how this is in part simple economics: "The more time teachers spend grading and conferencing, the less they are getting paid" (18).

WPA Advocacy

Recognizing that the research on class size has produced mixed results, especially around the impact of small class sizes on student retention, and that this work has been further complicated by a post-pandemic broad increase in drop rates, this study has focused more on WPA advocacy around class size and workload. There has been a rich history of WPAs exploring the ways they have successfully navigated institutional politics in advocating for their programs. In an oft-cited piece, Edward M. White makes the compelling case that WPAs often have more power than they think, and that powerlessness can be a mindset connected to our field's inherent aversion to the power structure and to wielding power. As White notes, a WPA resignation is often the worst-case threat to administration but often administrators are inclined to avoid that scenario because "A well-run composition program is a power base, since it frees administrators from what they fear most: constant harassment from discontented students and faculty" (11). Despite White's argument, Laura R. Micciche's feeling that the "WPA's authority and power are challenged, belittled, and seriously compromised every step of the way" (434) seems to be a more common feeling. As she and others illustrate, WPAs are often hired in more contingent positions that may not have the power of someone tenured nor the advantageous positionality of being a white male that White described. Moreover, as Andrea Dardello, Collin Lamont Craig, and Staci Perryman-Clark have detailed across various publications, BIPOC WPAs are likely to experience more scrutiny and challenging of their authority, having to do more work than white counterparts to establish their authority.

Making the similar argument that retaliation against WPAs is often invisible and also commonplace, Rita Malenczyk argues for a stronger alliance with the American Association of University Professors, as "historically it has had a good deal to do with how disciplinary expertise is perceived, honored, and protected" (22). Linda Adler-Kassner's (*Activist*; "Companies") work on advocacy among WPAs has been influential, especially her book *The Activist WPA*, in which she regularly references a Karl Llewellyn quote to argue that "Strategies without ideals is a menace, but ideals without strategies is a mess [sic]" (5). Explaining that WPAs are often up against powerful forces, she discusses a variety of strategies they can use to build alliances and reframe conversations to advocate their programs' interests. Similarly, Bruce Horner considers the importance of keeping our values as a central part of what we do and argues that we have to be strategic in how we invoke these values, lest we invoke values that "effectively undermine" our positions (163). Sticking to our values is all the more important and challenging in an era in which the neoliberalization of higher education has manufactured crises that have stripped programs and departments of their resources and has reduced the possibilities for true shared governance (Scott; Welch).

Throughout the past few decades, we have seen a variety of WPAs describe ways they have been strategic in advancing their programs, sometimes turning top-down state mandates into transformative work.

For instance, Rhonda Grego and Nancy S. Thompson narrate how they responded to their state's higher education commission's rejection of non-credit classes to create the studio model, a model that has become a staple in composition programs throughout the country. Elsewhere Heidi Estrem, Dawn Shepherd, and Samantha Sturman describe the problematic advocacy of Complete College America (CCA) and how they "were able to leverage the CCA 'game changer' into a change that mattered to us and to our students: replacing non-credit-bearing remedial courses with credit-bearing options that provide additional support" (60). Other WPAs discuss how they have drawn on kairotic moments at their own institutions to affect change. Kimberly Gunter narrates how a major revision of her institution's core curriculum, combined with a strong tradition of shared governance, enabled their program to shift away from an overwhelming dependance on adjunct labor to continuing faculty positions, with the latter expected to have greater expertise in rhetoric and composition. Of particular relevance to our study, she explained how advocacy for full-time positions has long been a central focus of her work: "low course caps matter little if faculty teach eight classes across three institutions, and professional development falters if only 20% of faculty attend workshops. Full-time lines, then, seemed to supersede everything" (65).

Methodology

The following research questions guided the collection and analysis of data for this study:

1. How do WPA and administrator orientations shape what arguments around workload and class size tend to be successful and unsuccessful?
2. How do contextual factors shape the ways WPAs make arguments around class size with administration?

Because of our stated interest in advocacy work, which is complex and deeply contextual, we determined that in-depth interviews instead of surveys were the most effective way of addressing our research questions. Analysis of interviews was combined with an analysis of written advocacy documents that participants were willing to share.

We initially recruited participants for this IRB-approved study (Protocol #1718003) through an open call on the Writing Studies listserv, which was followed by some targeted recruitment (through individual contacts as well the Teaching English in the Two-Year College listserv) aimed at increasing the representation of institution types. We conducted interviews with participants at twenty different institutions, which are listed in table 1.

Table 1
Participant Background]

Participant	Location	Type	Special Designation	Approximate Enrollment
Matthew	MW	regional state university (RSU)		20,000
Steve	MW	RSU		30,000
Andrew	MW	two-year college (TYC)		>50,000
Justin	MW	TYC		5,800
Dana and team (5 total)	MW	TYC		4,500
Lisa	MW	private liberal arts college (PLAC)		2,000
John	MW	Top-tier research university (R1)		40,000
Amy	S	RSU		20,000
Julie	S	RSU		35,000
Larry	S	private university (PU)		8,000
Paul	S	RSU	HBCU	3,000
Ethan	S	R1		33,000
Katherine	S	R1	HSI	>50,000
Kathy	W	TYC	HSI	7,500
Kurt	W	RSU	HSI	4,000
Laura	W	RSU		22,000
Madelyn	W	TYC		10,000
Frank	W	R1	HSI	30,000
Kevin	W	R1		>50,000
Jacob	W	TYC	HSI	20,000

As evident in table 1, we obtained decent geographical and institutional representation, interviewing WPAs at large nationally renowned research universities as well as two-year colleges of varying sizes. However, despite repeated attempts to reach out to WPAs at several HBCUs, we were only able to interview one participant from an HBCU, a point we raise in the discussion; similarly, we were not able to interview anyone at a Native Serving Institution, although Frank came from an institution that had a sizeable Native student population.

Interviews were conducted via Zoom, semi-structured, and included nineteen questions centered in three areas: general background, which asked about their experience and status at their particular institutions and general ways they have advocated for their programs; class size background, which solicited information on class sizes and workloads at their institutions and their attitudes towards smaller class sizes in general; and building arguments around class size, which focused on exploring the arguments they've made with administration about class size and what arguments have been more successful than others. Interviews lasted between forty-five and ninety minutes, with an average of sixty-five minutes.

Interviews were initially auto-transcribed by Zoom. We then listened to and edited transcripts for accuracy and identified some themes during this processing phase: kairos, campus culture, leadership norms, labor, departmental contradictions, administrative background, selective receptivity, regional culture, and faculty priorities. This list was developed deductively (by drawing on our aforementioned framework) and inductively (through the review of transcripts). As we re-read the transcripts, we identified passages that spoke to these themes and collated a list of these passages for each interview.

A Burkean Framework

The notion of worldview, or *weltanschauung*, has been a central frame for the analysis and presentation of data in this article. Kenneth Burke understood *weltanschauungen* as primarily linguistic phenomena and describes these distinct worldviews as "orientations." An orientation is a network of symbolic associations which Burke describes as "a bundle of judgements as to how things were, how they are, and how they may be" (*Permanence and Change* 14). For Burke, orientations arise as human beings habitually sort and classify experiences and behaviors by placing them into more general categories based on their resemblance to one another. Different groups will categorize experiences differently based on what each sees as the outstanding features of those experiences.

Burke holds that differences in orientation are primarily rooted in the material realities of sustenance and production. As different social groups and communities engage in different occupational methods of survival, unique, systematic approaches to life and its challenges arise. Burke describes these differences as "occupational psychoses," a term which describes how habits originally established in the context of specific occupations are "carried over into other aspects of . . . culture" (*Permanence and Change* 38). Thus, orientation displays a unique set of conceptual limitations which Burke dubs "trained incapacity," concerning which he observes that "A way of seeing is also a way of not seeing—a focus upon object A involves a neglect of object B" (*Permanence and Change* 49).

Although each orientation is uniquely fitted with a certain skill set to accomplish particular aims, there lies a temptation to apply that skill set to as many situations as possible. Thus, rival orientations come into conflict in their characterization of problems and their proposals for solutions. In historically remote times, this rivalry was, according to Burke, kept in check by the relatively limited number of different occupations (and consequently, orientations) within traditional societies. The modern period, however, exhibited an explosion of occupational diversity, which, in turn, demanded a universal language of value which could be implemented by societal leaders attempting to organize cooperative endeavors among subjects situated within different orientations. Money, being capable of representing and thus subsuming all other forms of value, has increasingly become the only value by which rival orientations can express ideas, concerns, goals, problems, and solutions to one another.

Although originally intended to serve as a point of mediation between rival orientations, we suggest that the neutralized, pragmatic language of "economic efficiency" which largely dominates institutional discourse today, and which easily justifies economic reductivism, has evolved into an orientation all of its own: neoliberalism. As we have seen, each orientation exhibits a "trained incapacity" in tending to apply its primary skill set to an ever-increasing range of situations, even those situations well beyond the original purview of the orientation's occupational basis (Burke, *Permanence and Change* 49). Neoliberalism, as a unique orientation, exhibits an impressive set of techniques and practices regarding managerial expertise and bureaucratic "efficiency," and yet has become incapable of appreciating rival values such as the humanist concerns for self-expression, civil responsibility, and personal wellbeing.

Findings

Navigating Occupational Psychosis in the Neoliberal University

As we conducted our interviews, it became immediately apparent that many WPAs were concerned about a phenomenon we have dubbed "neoliberal creep": the process by which campus culture and communications are gradually saturated with neoliberal language and thinking, a theme discussed by Welch and Scott. As a result of neoliberal creep, interactions between administrators, instructors, and students becomes increasingly transactional and businesslike, and administrators display an increased focus on marketing, branding, and the economic bottom line.

In this environment, WPAs struggle to have their own concerns heard; since their concerns are frequently rooted in a rival humanist orientation, these concerns are often normatively unintelligible to upper administrators. For instance, Andrew from a Midwest two-year college (TYC) recounted the way that upper administrators seemed unable to understand his viewpoint and rapidly translated his ethical appeals into an economic lexicon: "You're asking for fewer students, [and] I think sometimes what they hear is 'I want less work for the same pay' . . . . They want to quantify it that way, as opposed to starting with the position that . . . what we have now is broken." This intelligibility gap between rival paradigms is also a factor when considering pathetic rhetorical strategies. In another interview, John at a Midwest public R1 indicated that attempting to publicly shame his dean for a heartless indifference to quality of education proved fruitless: "[The shaming] button doesn't seem to work . . . it's all about the numbers with him." This minimization of humanist considerations, and a redirecting of attention to 'numbers,' was a theme addressed by multiple interviewees. Kurt, at a Hispanic-Serving Institution (HSI) RSU, recounted a similar scenario with his provost: "he goes 'I'm an engineer, I'm a numbers guy.' I've had people kind of mock [him] for it because he says it so much."

From multiple interviews, it seemed that administrators drawn from STEM fields might be particularly vulnerable to, or eager to employ, the neoliberal trope of reducing complex issues to numbers, which connects to Burke's description of the morally neutralized language of efficiency as a language "designed for machines" (*Permanence and Change* 58). This pattern, in turn, seems related to the low status of non-STEM fields generally. As Frank, from a public R1 HSI in the West, noted, "there's a tendency across academia and the rest of the world to mistrust the recommendations and the knowledge of other fields." Frank, like several other interviewees, refers to the resistance upper administrators displayed to the expertise and authority of writing studies scholarship. Hence, disciplinary sequestering, combined with the concentration of cultural capital in STEM fields, appears to further exacerbate the breakdown in communication between rival orientations in the academy. What results is the dominance of a morally impoverished language of valuation marshalled for neoliberal purposes. Utilizing a phrase that surfaced in multiple interviews, Dana and team from a Midwest TYC summarized the situation succinctly: "[Our administration] is all butts in seats and dollars in the bank."

It is evident that a neoliberal system perpetuates societal divides between the haves and have nots, which is manifested in the marginalization of HBCUs and TYCs and their students, as expressed by some participants. As Paul, from an HBCU in the South, noted, administrators at his institution counted on the fact that their largely first-generation college student population meant that several students would drop in the first part of the semester, reducing their real course sizes closer to twenty (from twenty-four) and ignoring arguments that instructors could possibly retain more students if starting at a lower cap. Paul's limited success in advocacy certainly stems in part from the position of his institution as an HBCU in a system that has traditionally and continues to place a lower value on BIPOC bodies. As he explained, "so we're definitely disadvantaged, I mean you go across town to [another public institution that serves more white students] and they're there at you know twenty-three students in comp to our twenty-six, well now twenty-five, and you have their faculty making ten grand a year less on average, same town you know." He explained the history of this campus across town, noting that it had been converted into a branch campus of a larger state institution, with that particular campus started in the 1940s to serve white students who did not want to attend school with Black students.

Similarly, it was evident that TYCs, which tend to serve higher percentages of first-generation students and BIPOC students, were often in marginalized positions compared to other state institutions. For instance, Jacob, working at a TYC in a reliably Democratic state in the West, noted that while he thought the CCCC recommendations were spot on, he said, "I am not at all confident or believe that they're realistic for my institution." He then detailed how the classes in the state flagship system, which serves the top students in the state, were capped at twenty-one, wondering why "does that top 10% then get like these smaller class sizes" when they are the "people who need it the least." Following Paul's comments above, we were also more likely to see larger class sizes justified at TYCs because students are expected to drop and bring the class sizes down.

Catherine Chaput has described the way branding has become a crucial technique of contemporary neoliberalism. This neoliberal enthusiasm for branding can leave WPAs quite literally disoriented, as recounted by Laura, at a Western RSU: "I was just from another meeting where they talked about the brand of GenED. Like, I guess I haven't really thought about our brand. Maybe I should have." Nonetheless, increasing considerations of branding can at times provide WPAs with opportunities for advocacy.

Elsewhere, Kurt (Western RSU HSI) described a period in which the upper administrators of his university were willing to lower class sizes for the sake of such branding: "They wanted that fodder for some like pamphlet or some web page or some commercial because, because, again with this whole revamping thing there's been a lot of like energy and action in that regard, like branding and creating materials and pointing to things like that." Thus, although the neoliberal focus on branding and advertisement rarely corresponds with the humanist goal of providing an excellent education, it can be important for WPAs to think critically about branding and both the threats and opportunities it poses for advocacy work.

In our interviews, we observed some WPAs attempting to thread the rhetorical needle by implementing *both* languages of value associated with the humanist and neoliberal orientations respectively. Julie, at a RSU in the South, noted, "I don't say standardization, either. I will say standardization for administration when they asked things. When I'm talking to faculty colleagues, I say consistency." On the other hand, Justin (Midwest TYC) was wary of employing the neoliberal language of valuation because it is a losing battle:

> Like let's say full time faculty have a slightly higher pass rate: it's never going to be high enough to justify the cost, if you look at it purely in terms of economics . . . it will always be cheaper to have an adjunct professor for $5,000 than it is a full-time professor for $75,000. Always, always, always. So, I don't want to I don't want to make it about money . . . because once we enter into the like "what's economically efficient [argument]," nope we've lost.

Thus, while it may be tempting for WPAs to do the work of translating their concerns and goals into the language of the neoliberal orientation, doing so can deprive their arguments of their authenticity and unique moral weightings, a concern expressed by Bruce Horner elsewhere. By relocating their appeals into the language of the neoliberal orientation, such WPAs would risk their arguments (and even their subjectivities) becoming neutralized and co-opted.

Another important factor to consider is when and how WPAs might cunningly force upper administrators to shift orientational lexicons. One example is given by Justin (Midwest TYC) as he describes efforts to lower the cap for remedial FYW courses. Justin recounts how he disingenuously and publicly stated the assumption that upper administrators held student learning as their highest priority, noting that "it's a— it's a way for us to kind of take the moral high ground and try to moralize and shame our administrators into decreasing the class sizes in the name of teaching [and] learning." Justin later indicated that although this move could be effective, its power might be depleted from overuse. In our estimation, in applying this strategy, WPAs might (if only momentarily) force upper administrators to conceptually inhabit an alternative orientation; and this may counter, or at least stall, the process of neoliberal creep. However, in estimating the broad applicability of this strategy, our optimism is tempered by considering John's earlier assertion that upper administrators have often so deeply internalized the neoliberal orientation so as to be un-shameable.

Unfortunately, this process of 'neoliberal creep' appears to be accelerating. John, at an institution with a president narrowly focused on keeping tuition costs low, described the way that his dean formed an alternative "shadow English department," run out of his own office, which supplied larger, inferior courses which met the requirements for FYW. John likens this process to Costco creating a cheaper Kirkland alternative:

> Walmart, Target, everyone does that, they'll have a competitor brand . . . well that's kind of what this this program is. It's like English department, you don't want to do this? We've got this competitor program over here that you know we're gonna run out of the dean's office so, you know. So they're always like well if you don't want to do it, we'll just add more sections over here. You know the thing is, though, students generally don't want to take a course like the one they're describing; they'd rather take an English course, but if they're mandated to take it, they will take it.

Thus, not only the language but also the managerial strategies of neoliberalism have begun to invade the university, yielding an ever-weakening bargaining position for faculty, and an inferior learning experience for students. It is noteworthy that John's dean employs a social scientist ethos to argue that he is data-focused, but, according to John, it is "clear that he is making arbitrary decisions." In short, administration can be dismissive of data when it works counter to their goals but happily make a claim to data when supporting them.

In sum, it quickly became apparent that WPAs conceived of and recounted their interactions with upper administrators in terms of rival worldviews, not only regarding class size and workloads but, more broadly, regarding the value and purpose of education and the university. WPAs consistently endorsed a humanist conception of education which emphasized the development of voice for the sake of communal and political participation. Contrarily, WPAs described upper administrators as committed to a notion of university success that minimized concerns about students' intellectual and cultural development, instead exhibiting a focus on bureaucratic and economic "efficiency" (i.e., a neoliberal approach).

WPA Rhetorical Strategies

As evident from the discussion in the previous section, WPAs learn to read the politics of their individual institutions and the values of those in managerial roles, conscious of adapting their discourses as they advocate for the various individuals in their programs. In this section, we would like to highlight some additional strategies that WPAs employed: identifying and building on administrative priorities, building partnerships across campus, recognizing that suffering should be shared, and drawing on community values.

Identifying and building on administrative priorities. WPAs have long been aware of their marginalized positioning in the institution and how their program advocacy is often ignored, even when backed with meaningful research and disciplinary recommendations that were included in a number of the documents that interviewees shared with us. As Paul (South HBCU) bluntly stated, "all the advocacy and all the stuff that I thought was very compelling didn't do a damn thing with the old guy." Similarly, Kathy at a TYC in the West explained that their "president is very strong and has made the decision that the financial aspects are what is most salient right now," and never anticipated having any traction on lowering class sizes without a change in leadership: "I think the advocacy is important, but I think, who we have in place administration-wise also makes such a difference." It is perhaps unsurprising then that several of our participants discussed the value of tying their class size and workload advocacy into broader administrative priorities, an approach that aligns with Burke's argument that persuasion happens primarily through identification: "You persuade a man [sic] only insofar as you talk his language . . . *identifying your ways with his*" (*A Rhetoric of Motives* 55).

For instance, Lisa at a Midwest private liberal arts college, explained how her institution was launching a new first-year studies program, and that the administration capped these courses at fifteen to incentivize people to teach them. New at the institution, she planned to "ride the coattails" of that initiative to argue for similar caps in all writing intensive courses. Elsewhere, Andrew (Midwest TYC) explained how two statewide task forces on composition success rates had made recommendations around class sizes and workloads but had limited success affecting change across campuses. However, the vice chancellor at his institution was inclined to try the recommended changes, in part because of another initiative happening at the same time: increasing the number of eight-week courses so students could take more courses in a given semester. As Andrew noted, "When that came out that was just a higher priority than everything else." He continued,

> there was an administrative concession made with our department which was "okay well when we start running these courses in this eight-week format, I will allow you to reduce the cap from twenty-four to eighteen." And then we were also able to squeeze in a reduction from twenty-four to twenty-one in the sixteen-week modality.

As Kurt noted in a different case, negotiations like these allow institutional leaders to take credit to other constituencies as they are able to trumpet the success of their initiatives: "the provost ended up bragging about the idea at the Board of Governors meeting." In a similar vein, some participants noted how administrators could be motivated by the boost to a *US News & World Report* ranking that comes with more classes at nineteen or fewer students or winning a particular award for innovation in education. Interest in these ratings or awards varied by institutional type, with WPAs from two-year colleges or regional colleges noting that their administrations tended to care little about national rankings.

Building partnerships across campus. Another strategy that several participants mentioned was building partnerships across campus. Matthew explained how their program worked with a variety of offices across campus, including the General Education Program, Office of Assessment, Institutional Research, and the Center for Innovative Teaching and Learning. These partnerships gave him more resources to demonstrate the impact of well-delivered small classes on student success, an argument that was successful when made in conjunction with others:

> Partnering with a number of other offices has really been crucial in saying well it's not just me and it's not just my discipline, the NCTE guidelines etc., CCCC. It's other units on campus all working actively to provide a framework that's institution-wide for what we do that shows that we're not in isolation and we're not just one hungry baby bird begging for resources.

Elsewhere, Andrew (Midwest RSU) explained how partnering with other programs could provide joint leverage in advocating for change. He explained how they formed an alliance with the Communications department as they lowered their course caps from thirty to twenty-one based on the argument that the need for so many students to deliver speeches really cut into instructional time. He focused in on student conferences in writing classes in making a similar argument. He furthered this argument by tying into administrative concerns over student success, noting that "forging those relationships between the instructor and the student was critical to ensuring that student success."

Another partnership that some people found valuable was with faculty unions, although these partnerships could go both ways, as some faculty defined equity narrowly. At one institution, Steve explained how the union was an asset in negotiating multi-year contracts for contingent faculty. However, both Madelyn and Justin, working at two-year colleges in different parts of the country, found that their unions failed to account for the nuance in workloads across disciplines. Madelyn explained,

> the union tries its best to say "all for one and one for all," but when you have a faculty teaching five classes or more, and the faculty member does not lecture nor does the faculty member read anything students write versus an English department faculty member who has to read some writing, there are great disparities.

Justin made a similar point when noting that the union was conscious about making smaller class sizes a constant part of negotiations (in part because he was on the negotiating team), but explained that the membership at large had limited concern about class sizes, often relegating this to a secondary priority: "How much are we going to fight about this and how much are we going to get hung up on it, especially when the membership at large doesn't seem to care as much."

Recognizing that suffering should be shared. Although writing teachers and administrators have a long history of placing concern for students at the center of their value systems, there was some recognition among WPAs that this has its limits and that our programs and faculty should not be the only ones bearing the impacts of unsustainable workloads. At a Midwest TYC, Dana and team noted that some of the advisors tended to exploit our field's student-centered values, sending students to the department to beg for seats in full sections with reasons such as they needed the course to stay on track for graduation. While they found it hard, the WPAs at that institution generally held firm in saying no. At a Midwest RSU, Matthew said his department chair was an ally in writing "amazingly perceptive emails to the dean" arguing how "We will push caps a bit, but we will not push them to irresponsible levels." In short, while their program may make some sacrifices to ensure students get into the classes they need, they will hold the ground at some point for both instructor wellness and quality of student learning.

Building on the unique situation provided by the COVID pandemic and the additional burdens it placed on faculty, Julie (RSU in the South) explained how she reduced the number of major writing assignments to help with faculty workload: "we want lower course caps and they say, well, we can't do lower course caps and then I said . . . let's pilot this at three assignments . . . that way, we have we have lower [number of] papers so it's a difference of . . . 130 papers." In selling this shift as a "pilot," she banked on the expectation that the administration would soon move onto other priorities: "they're not even looking at it anymore, they just wanted to know in the moment, so we will probably be able to keep that at three indefinitely." At the end of the day, she realized "they really didn't care about assignments—it was just a negotiating point for them."

Drawing on community values. Thus far we have conceptualized contentions between upper administrators and WPAs as taking place at intersection of two rival orientations: the neoliberal and humanist paradigms. In their advocacy, many WPAs spoke of difficulty in framing their arguments in a language of value which would not be simply co-opted by or mistranslated into the dominant language of the neoliberal orientation. From our interviews, we gathered that this effort is too much for any single rhetor. Interviewees spoke of the importance of grounding their appeals in reference to broader community values—it seems that situating such appeals within localized (non-neoliberal) orientations might lend WPAs added rhetorical ethos, buttressing what would otherwise be less formidable arguments.

Larry, at a private university in the South, emphasized making his own department a space wherein commitment to humanist values was the norm. To this end, Larry lauded hiring as a powerful advocacy strategy in that it allows WPAs to build intra-departmental consensus before moving on to upper admins: "When you can bring in people that are your sort of, that share your vision, advocacy gets easier and easier and easier because you're building up, building a consensus. When the . . . faculty were all together on something, then I knew I could move to the department and . . . gain consensus there and then move it up the chain."

The civic communities surrounding educational institutions were also considered crucial. Such communities are inevitably characterized by distinct moral and cultural norms. For example, the Midwest TYC where Justin worked was enmeshed within a region historically dominated by unionized labor and thus highly pro-union. This fact forced his administrators to tread carefully during union negotiations:

> it's just kind of taken for granted that there's going to be educational unions and they're just part of the landscape. Like our school our board of trustees is elected locally, and I'm sure it helps us that the

steel mills used to be big and there's generally . . . a fairly pro-union environment. I'm sure that helps because it means that the board doesn't even have to think about it, they don't have to think about union busting because they couldn't get away with it from their constituents, not only would they have to fight with us, but they would it would look bad.

In cases such as this, if administrators are perceived as going against a strongly held community value, then they could face serious resistance to their goals and consequently may tread more lightly than they would in a place where the community values align more closely with the administration's.

Discussion and Conclusion

In our analysis of these interviews, we have explored how WPA advocacy on class size often takes place at the intersection between two rival Burkean orientations: humanism and neoliberalism. Each orientation, in turn, expresses itself and makes claims to its preeminence in the university by way of its own characteristic language of valuation. Where the humanist orientation makes arguments concerning excellence in education and preparation for civic participation, the neoliberal orientation grounds its appeals in considerations of bureaucratic and economic "efficiency." Our participants illustrated how difficult it can be for WPAs to make effective arguments grounded in the humanist orientation and to drive upper administrators back from the neoliberal ruts they often find themselves in.

We saw how WPAs have generally avoided indiscriminately framing their arguments according to neoliberal principles, lest their arguments be co-opted and interpreted according to the neoliberal standards of valuation (and, as Justin pointed out, arguments for reasonable workloads and class sizes will never win in this frame). While some WPAs have either carefully threaded the rhetorical needle to employ each language of value when appropriate or have sought out crucial moments in which upper administrators could be forced to adopt the humanist language of value, other WPAs were able to position their own goals in relation to their administration's priorities, effectively employing embodied analogy to ride the coattails of prior initiatives. As Grego and Thompson illustrated with the creation of their studio model or Estrem, Shepherd, and Sturman illustrated with their placement system, sometimes building on the momentum of existing initiatives that we may in part find problematic can lead to innovative new approaches that align with our values.

As indicated above, we tried to interview participants across a variety of institution types in order to evaluate how advocacy varied across institutions. Whether in a progressive state in the West or a conservative state in the South, we saw funding disparities across institutional types that impacted advocacy work. As noted earlier, Paul (South HBCU RSU) clearly identified funding and class size disparities between his institution and a neighboring public institution that served more white students. This resonates with the realities that HBCUs continue to be marginalized within their systems, even compared to other public institutions in the same city (Adams and Tucker). We tried to interview more WPAs from HBCUs, but our emails went un-returned or, in one case, we had a signed consent form but failed to conduct an interview after almost three months of trying because the faculty were always overwhelmed with work. We feel this speaks to the likelihood that WPAs at HBCUs may be less supported than their counterparts at other institutions.

Similarly, as other work has documented, WPA roles at TYCs often have limited support—it is typically done by an informal committee of faculty, or the department chair, or even a dean (Snyder; Taylor), which was the case for our interviewees. In the case of the FYW committee we interviewed, they had the most protected person (i.e., a senior tenured faculty) take the group's recommendations forward to administration. Similarly, the course caps at TYCs were often higher than at more prestigious institutions, which came down in large part to funding disparities. As Jacob (West HSI TYC) noted, it is important to continue asking why the top students, arguably those who need the least amount of support, tend to have access to the smallest writing classes.

The results of advocacy, however, cannot be determined solely on institutional type, at least in a small-scale study such as this. Regardless of institutional type, campus leadership and their guiding values appeared to play a central role. For instance, John was at a major R1 university with a large amount of grant revenue where one of the president's main priorities was to keep tuition as low as possible. It is likely that no amount of rhetorical dexterity would have been able to prevent the dean from creating a cheaper product in lieu of their traditional FYW classes. As quoted earlier, Kathy (West HSI TYC) noted that their president emphasized budget cutting and never expected to make progress on lowering course caps without a change in leadership.

Despite some thorny ethical questions, we argue that the pain of high workloads and large classes imposed by states and institutions must be shared. Neoliberal administrators depend on our humanist orientations and disciplinary allegiances to press on with holding student conferences and giving extensive feedback on writing to best serve our students, even if it is unjust to and unsustainable for writing program faculty, many of whom are in contingent positions. We saw how Dana and team's refusal to admit extra students to course sections beyond course caps was seen as an act of solidarity with other instructors. In response to workload demands, Julie reduced the number of major writing assignments in their program. These strategies certainly come with ethical implications, especially since we have seen that class sizes and workloads at institutions that serve more marginalized student populations tend to be worse than their counterparts. Lowering the quality of instruction for these students helps perpetuate the divides wrought by neoliberalism. Nonetheless, the struggles to attract and retain faculty at such institutions is also an important consideration, not to mention that faculty at such institutions are more likely to come from marginalized groups themselves (Gasman; Smith, Tovar, and García).

Time and again, our participants expressed outrage at the fundamentally unethical way in which economic considerations were simply assumed to trump other metrics of value; at the same time, they consistently felt unheard and disempowered, unable to muster the institutional and cultural force necessary to dispute the primacy of the neoliberal orientation. As White notes, the threat of resignation or actual resignation is the ultimate weapon in a WPA's toolbox. Administrations might justly fear the collapse of a well-run composition program and may make concessions to avoid such an outcome. For instance, WPAs at institutions that have seen a lot of turnover in WPA roles may have more leverage to make demands and threats because administrators may be aware of how challenging it can be to maintain stability in the writing program. However, this strategy comes with some risk, as we saw at John's institution where the dean decided to dramatically shrink the program and pull it out of the English Department.

Overall, our participants broadly agreed that advocacy for FYW is not merely a matter of weighing the effectiveness of different administrative goals and methods, but rather is a contestation of normative ethics. John asserted that

> it's the ethics, you know . . . and I think that's your best move is to say this just on ethical [grounds] what you're doing here is you're loading more work on the TAs, more work on the lecturers, the quality of education is going to suffer.

It is evident that contesting the neoliberal orientation's domination of higher education tends to be too great a task for any one FYW program, and that other programs, institutions, and broader communities should be tapped as rhetorical resources and ethotic buttresses against the totalizing language of neoliberal valuation. As Scott and Welch remind us, budgetary crises are manufactured in the neoliberal system, so it is important to create spaces for genuine exchange and solidarity in order to collectively resist the oppressive nature of these systems. Through rhetorical dexterity, alliance building, and a patent refusal to continually increase workloads, we as WPAs can send the message to austerity-minded administrators that writing faculty will not continue to do more with less.

Works Cited

Adams, Susan, and Hank Tucker. "How America Cheated its Black Colleges." *Forbes*, 1 Feb. 2022, https://www.forbes.com/sites/susanadams/2022/02/01/for-hbcus-cheated-out-of-billions-bomb-threats-are-latest-indignity/?sh=6d6af7c2640c. Accessed 8 Oct. 2024.

Adler-Kassner, Linda. *The Activist WPA: Changing Stories About Writing and Writers*. UP of Colorado, 2008.

—. "The Companies We Keep or the Companies We Would Like to Try to Keep: Strategies and Tactics in Challenging Times." *WPA: Writing Program Administration*, vol. 36, no. 1, 2012, pp. 119–40.

Ake-Little, Ethan, Nathaniel von der Embse, and Dana Dawson. "Does Class Size Matter in the University Setting?" *Educational Researcher*, vol. 49, no. 8, 2020, pp. 595–605.

Bedard, Kelly, and Peter Kuhn. "Where Class Size Really Matters: Class Size and Student Ratings of Instructor Effectiveness." *Economics of Education Review*, vol. 27, no. 3, 2008, pp. 253–65.

Burke, Kenneth. *A Grammar of Motives*. California UP, 1945.

—. *A Rhetoric of Motives*. California UP, 1950.

—. *Permanence and Change*. California UP, 1954.

Chaput, Catherine. "Trumponomics, Neoliberal Branding, and the Rhetorical Circulation of Affect." *Advances in the History of Rhetoric*, vol. 21, no. 2, 2018, pp. 194–209.

CCCC Statement on Principles for the Postsecondary Teaching of Writing. CCCC, 2015, https://cccc.ncte.org/cccc/resources/positions/postsecondarywriting.

Cuseo, Joe. "The Empirical Case against Large Class Size: Adverse Effects on the Teaching, Learning, and Retention of First-Year Students." *The Journal of Faculty Development*, vol. 21, no. 1, 2007, pp. 5–21.

Dardello, Andrea. "Breaking the Silence of Racism and Bullying in Academia: Leaning into a Hard Truth." *Defining, Locating, and Addressing Bullying in the WPA Workplace*, edited by Cristyn L. Elder and Bethany Davila, Utah State UP, pp. 102–23.

Diette, Timothy M., and Manu Raghav. "Class Size Matters: Heterogeneous Effects of Larger Classes on College Student Learning." *Eastern Economic Journal*, vol. 41, no. 2, 2015, pp. 273–83.

Estrem, Heidi, Dawn Shepherd, and Samantha Sturman. "Reclaiming Writing Placement." *WPA: Writing Program Administration*, vol. 42, no. 1, 2018, pp. 56–71.

Gasman, Beth. "The Talent and Diversity of HBCU Faculty." *Forbes*, 19 July 2021, https://www.forbes.com/sites/marybethgasman/2021/07/19/the-talent-and-diversity-of-hbcu-faculty/#. Accessed 8 Oct. 2024.

Glau, Gregory R. "'Stretch' at 10: A Progress Report on Arizona State University's 'Stretch Program.'" *Journal of Basic Writing*, vol. 26, no. 2, 2007, pp. 30–48.

Grego, Rhonda, and Nancy S. Thompson. "The Writing Studio Program: Reconfiguring Basic Writing/Freshman." *WPA: Writing Program Administration*, vol. 19, no. 1–2, 1995, pp. 66–79.

Gunter, Kimberly. "Advocacy, Independence, and the Painful Kairotic Moment for Rhetoric and Composition." *WPA: Writing Program Administration*, vol. 43, no. 1, 2019, pp. 54–73.

Haswell, Richard H. "Class Sizes for Writing Courses—Regular, Advanced, Honors, and Basic For 310 Institutions." *CompPile*, Oct. 2015, http://comppile.org/profresources/classsize.htm.

Horning, Alice. "The Definitive Article on Class Size." *WPA: Writing Program Administration*, vol. 31, no. 1–2, 2007, pp. 11–34.

Horner, Bruce. "Redefining Work and Value for Writing Program Administration." *JAC*, vol. 27, no. 1/2, 2007, pp. 163–84.

Kokkelenberg, Edward C., Michael Dillon, and Sean M. Christy. "The Effects of Class Size on Student Grades at a Public University." *Economics of Education Review*, vol. 27, no. 2, 2008, pp. 221–33.

Lee, Melanie. "Rhetorical Roulette: Does Writing-Faculty Overload Disable Effective Response to Student Writing?" *Teaching English in the Two Year College*, vol. 37, no. 2, 2009, pp. 165–77.

Malenczyk, Rita. "Fighting Across the Curriculum: The WPA Joins the AAUP." *WPA: Writing Program Administration*, vol. 24, no. 3, 2009, pp. 11-24.

Micciche, Laura R. "More Than a Feeling: Disappointment and WPA Work." *College English*, vol. 64, no. 4, 2002, pp. 432–58.

Perryman-Clark, Staci. "Race, Teaching Assistants, and Workplace Bullying: Confessions from an African American Pre-Tenured WPA." *Defining, Locating, and Addressing Bullying in the WPA Workplace*, edited by Cristyn L. Elder and Bethany Davila, Utah State UP, pp. 124–37.

Phillips, Cassandra, and Greg Ahrenhoerster. "Class Size and First-Year Writing: Exploring the Effects on Pedagogy and Student Perception of Writing Process." *Teaching English in the Two Year College*, vol. 46, no. 1, 2018, pp. 9–29.

Queen, Bradley. "Class Size for a Multilingual Mainstream: Empirical Explorations." *WPA: Writing Program Administration*, vol. 40, no. 2, 2017, pp. 98–128.

Roberts-Miller, Patricia. "Class Size in College Writing (An Old Paper)." *Patricia Roberts-Miller*, 17 Oct. 2018, https://www.patriciarobertsmiller.com/2018/10/17/class-size-in-college-writing-an-old-paper/.

—. "Class Size and College Writing (Another Version of the Same Argument)." *Patricia Roberts-Miller*, 17 Oct. 2018, https://www.patriciarobertsmiller.com/2018/10/17/class-size-and-college-writing-another-version-of-the-same-argument/.

Scott, Tony. "Austerity and the Scales of Writing Program Administration: Some Reflections on the 2017 CWPA Conference." *WPA: Writing Program Administration*, vol. 41, no. 2, 2018, pp. 113–22.

Smith, Daryl G., Esau Tovar, and Hugo A. García. "Where are They? A Multilens Examination of the Distribution of Full-Time Faculty by Institutional Type, Race/Ethnicity, Gender, and Citizenship." *New Directions for Institutional Research*, vol. 155, 2012, pp. 5–26.

Snyder, Sarah Elizabeth. "Preparing to Become a Two-Year College Writing Program Administrator." *WPA: Writing Program Administration*, vol. 43, no. 3, 2020, pp. 106–20.

Taylor, Tim. "Writing Program Administration at the Two-Year College: Ghosts in the Machine." *WPA: Writing Program Administration*, vol. 32, no. 3, 2009, pp. 120–39.

Welch, Nancy. "'Everyone Should Have a Plan': A Neoliberal Primer for Writing Program Directors." *WPA: Writing Program Administration*, vol. 41, no. 2, 2018, pp. 104–12.

White, Edward M. "Use It or Lose It: Power and the WPA." *WPA: Writing Program Administration*, vol. 15, no. 1–2, 1991, pp. 3–12.

Wright, Mary C., Inger Bergom, and Tracy Bartholomew. "Decreased Class Size, Increased Active Learning? Intended and Enacted Teaching Strategies in Smaller Classes." *Active Learning in Higher Education*, vol. 20, no. 1, 2019, pp. 51–62.

Todd Ruecker is associate professor of English and Director of the University Composition Program at Colorado State University. His work regularly crosses disciplinary boundaries, and he has published articles in respected composition, education, and applied linguistics journals, including *TESOL Quarterly*, *College Composition and Communication*, and the *Journal of Educational Policy*. He has served as an editor of the *Journal of Second Language Writing* and has published a monograph and several edited collections.

Galen Gorelangton is a doctoral candidate in rhetoric and writing studies in the Department of English at the University of Nevada, Reno. His research interests include virtue ethics, religious rhetoric, and disability studies. This article is his first publication in a peer-reviewed academic journal—future research projects will explore Buddhist rhetorics (especially those of the *Jodo Shinshu* tradition) and ways that Buddhist mindfulness practices can enrich college composition classrooms.

Are We Preparing Students to Write across the Curriculum?: An Analysis of Learning Outcomes for First-Year Composition at Two-Year Colleges

Teresa Thonney

Abstract

At two-year colleges, English composition courses focus on skills students need to write across the curriculum, yet there is limited evidence that students successfully transfer those skills when writing in other classroom contexts. In this article, I compare the skills taught in first-year composition to the skills students need to write across the curriculum and discuss ways to help students transfer what they've learned in their composition course to new writing contexts.

At two-year colleges, most degree-seeking students take first-year composition (FYC), a general writing course often, but not always, taken during the first year of college. This course is "where students develop the advanced literacy skills needed to succeed in courses in other disciplines" (Nazzal, Olson, and Chung 264). Indeed, the primary justification for the (nearly) universal first-year composition course requirement is the assumption that the skills taught there can be applied in other contexts, including writing for other courses (Blaauw-Hara 354; Tinberg 7–8). Yet, as Howard Tinberg concluded from interviews with community college faculty, many English instructors know little about the writing assigned outside the English department (28), which raises a question: Do English composition courses teach the skills students need to successfully write in other general education courses?

In this article, I examine three questions: (1) What skills are typically taught in FYC?; (2) What skills are needed for writing across the curriculum?; and (3) If the skills taught in FYC are the skills needed to write in other disciplines, how can we help students transfer what they've learned in FYC to other contexts? For WPAs, FYC coordinators, and others involved in FYC curriculum development, this study provides insights into how their own FYC learning outcomes compare to those of other colleges, how the skills taught in their FYC courses align with the skills students need to write in other courses, and how FYC can be designed to help students transfer what they learn to new writing contexts.

Student Learning Outcomes in First-Year Composition Courses

To determine the focus of FYC, I reviewed catalog descriptions and student learning outcomes from a sample of two-year colleges across the country.

Methods

Student learning outcomes identify the knowledge and skills a student should have after completing a course. My original goal was to survey FYC learning outcomes for community colleges but not technical colleges because at some technical colleges FYC focuses on workplace writing. However, Delaware, South Carolina, and Wisconsin have few or no community colleges. Therefore, technical colleges from those states are included in the sample to ensure representation from all fifty states.

Using alphabetized and then numbered lists of public two-year schools for each state and Google's random number generator, I selected approximately one-quarter of the colleges in each state. All colleges in the sample offer AA, AS, or AAS degrees but few if any BA degrees. The sample includes 221 colleges, eighteen of them technical colleges: 110 small colleges (<5,000 students), fifty-nine medium-sized colleges (5,000–9,999 students), twenty-four medium-large colleges (10,000–15,000 students), and twenty-eight large colleges (15,000+ students).

For each college, the lowest-level credit-bearing general writing course was selected—the course required for most degree-seeking students. When learning outcomes for this course were not available on a college's website, English department faculty were emailed. However, not all responded. For these colleges, my analysis is limited to the FYC catalog description. In the end, both FYC catalog descriptions and learning outcomes were analyzed for 164 colleges (74% of the sample); course catalog descriptions alone (without learning outcomes) were analyzed for another fifty-seven colleges (26%).

After identifying recurring topics, I re-read the catalog descriptions and learning outcomes and coded relevant information with the appropriate category name. Through this process, the most common FYC skills across the sample were identified (see table 1).

There are limitations to my methods for determining what is taught in FYC: (1) For fifty-seven colleges, I analyzed only FYC catalog descriptions, which do not identify all of the skills taught in a course. This means some results in table 1 underestimate reality. (2) Outcome statements do not reveal the extent to which each skill is emphasized nor do they convey the level of skill required of students. For example, "integrating source information" is a common FYC outcome, but there is considerable difference between asking students to find, interpret, and summarize sources on their own and providing students with sources that are then summarized for them in class. (3) It's also possible that, in some English departments, outcome statements do not drive instruction or assessment in any consistent manner. However, given their prominence in course syllabi, learning outcome statements likely reflect what's happening in most classrooms.

Findings

Table 1 lists skills mentioned in a majority of FYC catalog descriptions or learning outcomes in the sample.

Table 1
Most commonly mentioned skills in catalog descriptions and student learning outcomes for first-year composition courses (N = 221)

Skill or Focus in First-Year Composition	Number of Schools	Percentage of Schools
Analysis of texts, critical reading, or critical thinking	202	91%
Integrating source information (summary, paraphrase, quotation)	193	87%
Writing process (plan, write, revise, edit)	176	80%
Analyzing rhetorical situations or writing for different audiences and purposes	160	72%
Essay writing	158	71%
Formal documentation (MLA or APA)	158	71%
Research/locating sources	158	71%
Standard written English	143	65%
Reference to "academic writing," "academic discourse," "academic writing conventions," "writing across disciplines," "college writing/composition," "college-level"	142	64%
Organization	132	60%

Catalog descriptions and learning outcomes indicate that FYC is not so much a "general writing" course as an "introduction to academic writing" course. More than half of the FYC skills listed in table 1 are academic skills: analysis, conducting research, integrating source information, documenting source information, and essay writing. (Writing process, analyzing rhetorical situations, using standard written English, and effective organization, conversely, are more universal writing skills.) Keyword searches conducted on the corpus of catalog descriptions and outcome statements reflect the emphasis on activities associated with academic writing, including reading, analysis, research, and working with sources.

Reading and analysis. Throughout the corpus, it's evident that FYC focuses not only on writing but also on reading as an integral part of the composing process. The references to reading (298 instances) include eighty-one references to "reading critically," "critical reading," "close reading," or "analytical reading." "Critical thinking" appears in seventy-six course descriptions, but "analysis" ("analyze" or "analyzing") is even more prevalent, appearing 282 times in the corpus, almost always in reference to analyzing texts, arguments, or essays, but also sometimes referring to analyzing audiences or rhetorical situations.

Research and writing from sources. "Evaluate" (or "evaluating") also appears frequently (204 instances), usually referring to evaluating sources, information, or evidence. Evaluating sources is one of several ways research skills are emphasized throughout the corpus. The word "research" appears 293 times, and "source" appears 290 times. Learning to use library resources is mentioned forty-seven times.

Using source information to develop papers is mentioned in 87% of the course descriptions (including fifty-nine references to synthesizing sources). Formal documentation of source information is referred to in 71% of the learning outcomes. There are also twenty-six references to plagiarism and forty-three references to using sources ethically or responsibly.

Academic writing. Analysis, research, and working with sources are all academic writing skills, but the most obvious indication that FYC emphasizes academic writing is the many explicit references to academic or college writing. The word "academic" appears 222 times in the corpus, usually referring to "academic writing" or "academic discourse." There are also references to "academic essays," "academic tone," "academic English," "academic audience," "academic conventions," "academic research," "academic documentation," "academic sources," and "academic genres." References to "college" are common as well. FYC is called "College Composition" or "College Writing" at twenty-eight schools in the sample, and "college-level" appears eighty-eight times in the corpus, usually referring to writing "college-level essays" or producing "college-level writing."

Statements identifying academic writing as the focus of FYC are found throughout the corpus, as demonstrated in the examples below (taken verbatim from the corpus). According to these statements, FYC:

- prepares the student for the exposition, analysis, and argument required in college writing.
- provides practice in producing substantial compositions at the college transfer level for courses across the curriculum.
- prepares students for the demands of college level writing.
- provides instruction and practice in reading, researching, and writing for college.

These findings mirror those of Dylan Dryer, who, after analyzing grading rubrics from first-year writing programs at eighty-three US universities, determined that FYC courses are "designed to introduce [students] to the conventions of academic writing" (4), including explicitly announced thesis and organization, use of appropriate evidence, critical thinking and analysis, audience and rhetorical awareness, and an acceptable mastery of grammar and genre conventions (12).

Writing across the Curriculum in Two-Year Colleges

Course descriptions indicate that FYC at two-year colleges is designed to prepare students for writing in college. But does FYC focus on the actual skills students need when writing in other courses? For insights into what skills are needed to write across the curriculum, I turned to faculty surveys and studies of student writing. For example, Mark Blaauw-Hara invited the twenty-five full-time faculty who taught outside the writing program at his community college to submit representative writing assignments from their courses. He received assignments from fifteen full-time faculty, including from math, social sciences, physical sciences, and nursing, and he later gathered seventeen additional assignments from adjunct faculty. Three-fourths of the thirty-two assignments require integrating information from sources. Critically evaluating sources is required in 47% of the assignments, and description is required in 44% (357–58). When I asked twenty-six instructors at my own community college for samples of student writing, seventeen instructors, representing eleven disciplines, submitted writing from their courses. In a majority of the papers, sources are cited, and all of them include interpretation of data or analysis. For instance, in chemistry and microbiology, students interpret experiment results, in geography they interpret seismograph readings, in abnormal psychology they interpret patient symptoms, and in statistics they interpret data about a sample. Other assignments involve analyzing a text, performance, or film (Thonney, "'At First'").

Howard Tinberg and Jean-Paul Nadeau interviewed eleven faculty from across the curriculum at their community college. Their assignments require observation (agency field reports and ethnographies), analysis (of films or business operations), and description and evaluation (nursing care plans) (39). In a survey of faculty at the same college, 69% of the 70 respondents indicated that they assign research writing (Tinberg and Nadeau 41). More than half of the twenty-three community college instructors responding to Julia Carroll and Helene Dunkelblau's survey teach social sciences, business, history, or nursing courses. Seventy percent of the respondents assign essays, and nearly half assign research papers (274–76).

In a national survey of non-composition instructors at two-year colleges, 77% of the 171 respondents, representing 140 colleges and fifteen disciplines, said they assign extended writing (defined as two or more pages). These assignments require integration of source material (mentioned by 79%), analysis (mentioned by 72%), personal response to course concepts or application of course concepts (mentioned by 56%), and source summary with evaluation or response (mentioned by 55%) (Thonney, "What Community"). Among the 104 community college students in New York who participated in a study for psychology research credit, 24% had written 1–4 papers during the current term, 42% had written 5–10 papers, and 23% had written 11–20 papers. Synthesis of source information was, on average, required in three papers during the term (Ahmed 43).

These faculty and student surveys indicate that skills taught in FYC—analysis, locating sources, and writing from sources—are skills students need to write across the curriculum. Further evidence for this conclusion can be found in writing assignment prompts from general education courses. To locate writing assignments from community college courses, I conducted keyword searches (combining, for example, "writing," "student writing," or "writing assignments" with "community colleges" or "two-year colleges") in library databases and in various teaching journals (such as *American Biology Teacher* and *Teaching Sociology*). My search produced thirty publications that included detailed assignment descriptions from courses in agriculture, business, education, engineering, history, mathematics, life sciences, physical sciences, and social sciences. (A sampling of these assignments appears in the appendix.) Together, they demonstrate that writing in general education courses at two-year colleges typically requires analysis or critical thinking (all thirty assignments) and integrating information from sources (twenty-four of thirty assignments). In addition, at least one-third of the assignments require students find their sources. (In the other source-based assignments, it is unclear if sources are provided or if students locate sources themselves.)

Discussion and Recommendations

The literature reviewed in the previous section indicates that the skills needed to write across the curriculum at two-year colleges are skills taught in FYC, including locating sources, reading and evaluating sources, summarizing sources, citing sources, analysis, and critical thinking. Yet, despite the similarities in writing for FYC and writing for other courses, evidence that community college students transfer skills learned in FYC to other contexts is difficult to find. Dianne Fallon, Cindy Lahar, and David Susman analyzed psychology research papers that were "quite similar to what we might ask of students in the first-year writing course" (42), but previously taking FYC had no bearing on how students scored (44). Thomas Martin, who analyzed papers written for philosophy, government, history, and humanities, determined that completion of FYC was an "inconsistent predictor of student performance."

Indeed, two-year college faculty across the curriculum say students are underprepared for the writing they assign. Non-composition faculty ($N = 177$) responding to a national survey identified critical thinking/analysis, finding credible sources, integration of source material, formal documentation, organization, using standard written English, and familiarity with academic writing conventions as skills many students lack (Thonney, "What"). These same skills are among the most commonly mentioned in FYC descriptions. In a faculty survey at three New York community colleges, 68% of respondents ($N = 420$) described students' reading and writing skills as "weak or deficient" (Schrynemakers, Lane, Beckford, and Kim 19). Similarly, 89% of faculty responding to a survey by Tinberg and Nadeau ($N = 70$) believed their students are unprepared for challenging writing tasks (39; see also Bunch, Schlaman, Lang, and Kenner).

If most two-year college students take FYC and if FYC teaches the skills students need to successfully write in college, why isn't there more evidence of students demonstrating these skills when writing for general education courses? There are a number of possible explanations. Students may not take writing seriously in courses that are not composition courses (Thonney, "What"), or faculty whose focus is not on writing may not provide sufficient time or support for students to produce their best writing (Nelms and Dively 216; Wardle 76). And, of course, many students enroll in college-credit, general education courses before they've taken English composition. Another obstacle to transfer, explain Linda Bergmann and Janet Zepernick, is that many students regard writing in composition courses as "personal, subjective, creative," and unlike the "objective, fact-based" writing they do in other courses (131; see also Jarratt et al. 51, 61).

Students don't look for opportunities to use skills learned in FYC "because they believe that skills learned in FYC have no value in any other setting" (Bergmann and Zepernick 139).

In order to apply what they've learned in one situation to another, students must recognize similarities in writing tasks (James 95). But undergraduates write many types of papers, such as laboratory reports, proposals, reviews, science posters, and design specifications. As a result, students may not recognize when they can apply skills they've previously learned. Even familiar genres may not look the same in different contexts. Research papers written for science courses, for example, often include section headings, figures, and tables, but these features are rarely found in research papers written for FYC. Higher-order skills can also look different in different contexts. Analysis of numerical data, for instance, bears little resemblance to the analysis of texts students do in FYC. Reading comprehension skills are not always generalizable either. Proficient readers in English courses, for instance, may struggle understanding biology texts because of unfamiliar concepts, vocabulary, and genres (Thonney, "Analyzing" 393).

It's also possible that an English department's outcome statements do not reflect what's being emphasized in specific FYC courses. For example, if more time is spent discussing political or cultural issues than discussing academic writing skills, students may remember a particular political or cultural topic as the "subject" of FYC rather than writing itself (Fulkerson 663; Yancey, Robertson, and Taczak 83), in the same way a student might remember a writing-intensive history class as a history class with writing "tacked on" (Jarratt, Mack, Sartor, and Watson 51). Nor do outcome statements reveal the competency level required of students. As already noted, students asked to summarize sources previously summarized for them in class discussions have not actually demonstrated an ability to understand or interpret sources. Tinberg identifies additional factors that "inhibit efforts to teach to and for transfer" (29), including dependence on overworked contingent faculty, reduced funding for professional development, elimination of course prerequisites, and scarcity of writing-intensive courses in the disciplines (28–29).

Nevertheless, most FYC instructors invest considerable time helping students develop the skills needed to write in other courses. How, then, can WPAs support faculty efforts to prepare students to transfer and repurpose those skills when writing in other academic contexts?

Discuss Transfer with Faculty

Despite the obvious benefit of helping students understand how their learning can be applied beyond a single classroom, few college courses have learning transfer as a course objective. That this is the case for FYC, in particular, is noteworthy given that learning transfer has been a subject of interest in composition studies for decades, and preparing students for college writing is a goal of most FYC courses (at least those represented in the sample). Although both "writing process" and "analyzing rhetorical situations" are typically taught in FYC, adapting to new contexts and genres appears less often in course descriptions and learning outcomes. Only 14% of colleges in the sample (N = 221) mention writing across the curriculum or in other disciplines; only 24% mention reading or writing various genres. This matters because, as Jessie Moore concluded after reviewing the body of writing-related transfer research, most students on their own don't recognize how what they learn in FYC applies to their writing in other courses (also Jarratt, Mack, Sartor, and Watson). Even among students who think FYC prepared them for writing in other courses, as the community college students Tinberg surveyed (N = 110) overwhelmingly did, few can identify specific knowledge beyond grammar, essay structure, and source citation that they could transfer from FYC to writing in other courses, suggesting that their FYC curriculum emphasized "correctness" and grammar but not how to approach new genres and writing contexts (13, 15–16). If preparing students for college writing is a key purpose of FYC, learning transfer should be identified in course catalog descriptions, student learning outcomes, and class discussions.

Another potential obstacle to transfer is faculty attitudes and awareness. Many FYC instructors know little about the writing assigned across the curriculum, and what faculty outside of English departments know about FYC is often just as limited (Tinberg 28). As a result, FYC instructors don't know how best to prepare students for what's ahead, and instructors in other disciplines do not build on students' prior knowledge. Dorothy Worden-Chambers and Ashley Montgomery note that efforts to adopt a transfer-focused curriculum in FYC can fail if there are "mismatches between the values of the curriculum and teachers' beliefs" (131). They suggest WPAs who want to facilitate transfer should first learn about and then build on teachers' current understanding of what transferable skills can and should be taught (131).

WPAs can expand faculty understanding of what transferable skills can be taught in FYC by surveying the writing assigned on their campuses. At my community college, I gathered student papers from across the curriculum that had been assigned an "A" grade—thirty-one papers from courses outside the English department and two from literature courses. After obtaining permission from the authors, these papers and corresponding assignment prompts were compiled into a digital library, used for FYC class discussions, for short writing assignments, and as sources for textual analysis writing projects. The papers reveal many similarities, such as the inclusion of a central claim, analysis of evidence, integration of source material, and source citations. Just as important, however, they reveal differences. For example, most of the thirty-three student papers include information from sources, but only literature papers include quotations; most papers include source citations, but only in art history and literature is MLA format used; most papers are essays, but many of the essays include section headings and tables or figures. All papers include analysis, but analysis of numerical data or observations is more common than analysis of texts. FYC instructors familiar with the writing assigned at their colleges understand what writing features students can transfer or repurpose from FYC, as well as what features students may need to abandon in other contexts.

WPAs can further facilitate transfer through all-faculty workshops. Workshops, for example, can teach faculty across the curriculum how to build on students' prior writing knowledge. Dave Kim and Wendy Olson describe how engineering faculty at one university used vocabulary taught in FYC (e.g., "audience," "claims," "evidence," "sources," "genre conventions") when introducing a new genre: the engineering lab report (68). Compared to students in a control group, students instructed in this rhetorical approach demonstrated greater understanding of audience and style in their writing (81). Most students need additional support when they encounter new genres or rhetorical situations (Sommers and Saltz 145; Faulkner 45); using writing terms students have previously learned can provide this support. Lisa Shaver recommends creating assignment titles that name the required skill or genre and—at least within a given department—being consistent in use of terms so that students can recognize when a new writing assignment is similar to previous writing or, conversely, when an assignment requires skills or genres new to them (87). In Shaver's study, students given an assignment titled "Executive Summary" could make connections to previous writing they had done; they could not do the same for an assignment titled "Cross-Border Merger" (84–86). In workshops at his community college, Blaauw-Hara has taught faculty how to design clear writing prompts. He suggests using a similar layout and structure for assignment prompts across campus to "help students see the similarities between writing contexts and help us cue for transfer" (359). By learning about the writing assigned at their college and designing assignments to cue for transfer, all faculty can help students apply skills learned in FYC to other contexts.

Design FYC to Facilitate Transfer

Designing the FYC curriculum to cue for transfer can change the perception of FYC being unrelated to a student's broader education. Dolores Perin, discussing students in developmental writing courses, argues that making connections between the skills taught in writing courses and the skills needed to write in other courses can motivate students "to persist in learning skills that normally are not, in themselves, of great interest to them" (137). In FYC courses, motivation to learn transferable skills is potentially greater still because most students are concurrently enrolled in other credit-bearing courses. While it's true that successfully transferring writing skills from one context to another requires time and practice across the curriculum, FYC courses can lay the groundwork by teaching students how to approach new genres and teaching skills students can use in other writing contexts.

Previous research has demonstrated the value of a transfer-focused FYC pedagogy. Kathleen Yancey, Liane Robertson, and Kara Taczak followed seven university students who had taken FYC taught in one of three pedagogical approaches: expressivist (personal reflection writing and writing about cultural identity), media and cultural studies (writing about media or culture), or teaching for transfer, featuring assignments designed to promote metacognition. Students in the teaching for transfer section reflect on how rhetorical situations and genres are alike or different, consider how they could adapt their writing knowledge to new situations, and write various genres (57–58). Compared to students in the other FYC sections, students who had taken the transfer-focused course were better able to analyze audience and purpose, analyze genre expectations, and adapt prior knowledge in their future assignments (95–99). (The authors provide course schedules and writing prompts for their teaching for transfer curriculum. In addition, Sonja Andrus, Sharon Mitchler, and Howard Tinberg describe how they modified the curriculum for FYC in two-year colleges.) James Pacello, who interviewed students enrolled in a developmental English course focused on transfer, also describes the value of a transfer-focused pedagogy.

Other researchers have linked writing development to understanding how writing is shaped by audience, purpose, and genre (Negretti 173). Tanzina Ahmed found that the better students are at adapting their writing to new audiences, genres, and situations, the higher their GPA, leading her to conclude that introducing community college students to various genres is crucial to their development as writers (60, 68–69). Dana Driscoll et al. agree. After gathering surveys, interviews, reflective writing, and sample papers from over 450 university students enrolled in general writing courses, they concluded that more than any other factor, genre awareness—specifically, understanding how a genre's conventions help accomplish a writer's goals and fulfill audience expectations—correlated with improvement in students' writing across the semester (84). The authors recommend various activities to develop genre awareness, including writing for diverse audiences, analyzing sources to determine intended audience and purpose, and noticing how authors join an existing conversation (94).

Students who leave FYC aware of genre variation understand that learning new conventions is part of learning how to communicate in new contexts. As one student explained, after taking a transfer-focused FYC course: "Once you understand that different genres are meant to do different things for different audiences you know more about writing that works for whatever context you're writing in" (qtd. in Yancey, Robertson, and Taczak 95). An engineering student similarly describes the cumulative effect of writing varied genres: When "you experience many kinds of writing . . . the process of learning how to write the new format is faster because you already switched once" (qtd. in Jarratt, Mack, Sartor, and Watson 66). This level of developmental maturity emerges after extensive practice and reflection, but it can be fostered in FYC through exposure to various rhetorical situations.

George Bunch suggests having students analyze varied academic texts through the lens of "metagenre" (178), Michael Carter's term for different ways of knowing in academic disciplines: problem solving, empirical inquiry, research from sources, and performance (176). Another approach is to have students analyze how aspects of style, organization, and source citation vary. Questions to guide students' analysis of academic texts might include: What is the purpose of the paper? What purposes does the introduction serve? Are there section headings? If so, how do they help readers? Who appears to be the intended audience? What kind of evidence is provided? Are there figures or tables? If so, what purpose do they serve? What kinds of information appear within in-text citations, and what are the benefits of providing that information for readers? Writing prompts from across the curriculum can also be used to show students other writing contexts. Ann Johns provides questions to help students analyze writing prompts (244). An FYC curriculum that introduces students to writing from various disciplines introduces them to "different ways that problems are articulated, different kinds of data that are brought to bear on those problems, and different ways of interpreting evidence and making claims" (Bunch, Schlaman, Lang, and Kenner 322).

If the goals of FYC include preparing students to write in college, then reading, citing, and finding connections between texts should also be at the heart of the curriculum because most college writing assignments involve integration of source material. Joining a conversation among published authors is daunting for any novice, but all the more so for students with no experience reading academic texts. A temptation in this situation can be to summarize sources in class discussion. In fact, in one survey of community college students, nearly 70% of respondents ($N = 447$) said their instructors explained assigned reading at least 50% of the time (Armstrong, Stahl, and Kantner 897). Instead of letting students rely on others to interpret texts (or avoid reading altogether), John Bean and Dan Melzer recommend teaching students how to approach difficult texts and making them accountable for reading them. In chapter seven of their book *Engaging Ideas*, Bean and Melzer suggest methods and writing assignments to develop reading skills. Additional assignments are described by Jaclyn Hilberg. Her classroom activities ask students to reflect on their current reading strategies; to consider how they might, depending on their purpose, revise their reading strategies; and to consider ways to strategically adapt their reading practices to assignments across the curriculum.

Finally, the FYC curriculum can facilitate transfer by introducing writing conventions valued by faculty across disciplines, such as announcing the topic and organization of a paper (Bahls, Mecklenburg-Faenger, Scott-Copses, and Warnick; Miller and Pessoa 862–64), responding to contrasting evidence or viewpoints (Miller, Mitchell, and Pessoa 115), using hedges to qualify claims (Lee and Deakin 27; Uccelli, Dobbs, and Scott 49), using organizational markers (Uccelli, Dobbs, and Scott 49), and using reformulation markers, such as "in other words" and "specifically" (Aull and Lancaster 164–65). These writing conventions can be transferred to many writing contexts, and instruction in their use conveys a principle new to many first-year students: that a writer's goal is not only to demonstrate understanding of the subject but also to guide readers, reiterate information, and mitigate potential for misunderstanding.

Conclusion

In this article, I have shown considerable overlap in the skills taught in FYC and the skills needed to write across the curriculum. Yet, there is limited evidence that community college students successfully apply skills learned in FYC to their writing in other courses. This may be due in part to the inherent difficulty of documenting transfer of writing skills (Jarratt, Mack, Sartor, and Watson); it's also undoubtedly because measurable writing development emerges over time. This is true for well-prepared students and especially true for students who enter FYC lacking basic skills related to reading, organization, and language use. However, by revising FYC learning outcomes to focus more explicitly on transfer, a first-year composition program can lay important groundwork by teaching students how to analyze new writing situations and how to apply and adapt what they learn in FYC to writing across the curriculum.

Appendix: Examples of Writing Assignments across the Curriculum at Two-Year Colleges

Table 2. Examples of Writing Assignments across the Curriculum at Two-Year Colleges. * Indicates that the article includes the writing assignment prompt and/or grading rubric.

Course	Assignment	Skills Required	Source
Algebra	Essay on how culture influenced the student's career choice, using sources and quantitative data students calculate	Reading, synthesizing sources, quantitative reasoning, interpretation of data	Boumlik, Jaafar, and Alberts*
Biology	Essay describing ecological dilemmas, followed by recommendations	Summary and response, considering different perspectives	Balgopal, Wallace, and Dahlberg*
Biology	Research paper about DNA fingerprinting or genetic differences between individuals or groups	Locating and evaluating sources, synthesizing sources, citations/bibliography	Kim, Franco, and Seo
Botany	Paper connecting prior experiences with plants to biology concepts	Analysis and making connections between old and new information	Wandersee, Clary, and Guzman*
Chemistry	Report with abstract, research question, methods and observations, graphs, and conclusions	Designing research study, preparing samples, analyzing and presenting results, citations/bibliography	Kim, Roth, and Zhang
Economics	Report describing a country's economic performance and economic forecast, with recommendations	Locating sources, synthesizing sources, analyzing data, citations/bibliography	Tila*
Engineering Technology	Research paper about innovative technology and sustainability	Locating and evaluating sources, synthesizing sources, citations/bibliography	Kim, Franco, and Seo
History	Report describing interview of a primary source	Interviewing, summarizing, quoting, synthesizing sources, citations/bibliography	Perrotta*

124

Table 2. cont.

Course	Assignment	Skills Required	Source
History	Summary and critical analysis of primary sources	Rhetorical analysis (summary, quotation, evaluation)	Tinberg*
Liberal Arts Seminar	Research paper with background, discussion, and conclusions about women's contributions in science	Locating sources, summarizing, quoting, citations/bibliography	Boumlik, Jaafar, and Alberts*
Marine Biology	Report describing research question, hypothesis, methods, and results	Hypothesis development, collecting, analyzing, and interpreting data, presenting results, citations/bibliography	Rosas Alquicira et al.
Psychology (General)	Proposal describing hypothesis and experiment design, supported with evidence from research studies	Experimental design, locating sources, synthesizing sources, citations/bibliography	Tinberg*
Psychology (Human Development)	Paper describing interview subjects of various ages using Erikson's Theory of Psychosocial Development	Interviewing, synthesizing sources, analysis	Varelas, Wolfe, and Ialongo*
Sociology	Research project connecting worksite observations and interviews to course content on culture and racial/gender disparities in chosen professions	Observation, interviewing, analyzing fieldnotes and interview transcripts, interpreting government data, statistical analysis	Traver
Statistics	Evaluation of a statistical study	Locating sources, summary, data analysis	Estrada*

Works Cited

Ahmed, Tanzina. "'Helping Me Learn New Things Every Day': The Power of Community College Students' Writing across Genres." *Written Communication*, vol. 38, no. 1, 2021, pp. 31–76.

Andrus, Sonja, Sharon Mitchler, and Howard Tinberg. "Teaching for Writing Transfer: A Practical Guide for Teachers." *Teaching English in the Two-Year College*, vol. 47, no. 1, 2019, pp. 76–89.

Armstrong, Sonya L., Norman A. Stahl, and M. Joanne Kantner. "Building Better Bridges: Understanding Academic Text Readiness at One Community College." *Community College Journal of Research and Practice*, vol. 40, no. 11, 2016, pp. 885–908.

Aull, Laura L., and Zak Lancaster. "Linguistic Markers of Stance in Early and Advanced Academic Writing: A Corpus-Based Comparison." *Written Communication*, vol. 31, no. 2, 2014, pp. 151–83.

Bahls, Patrick, Amy Mecklenburg-Faenger, Meg Scott-Copses, and Chris Warnick. "Proofs and Persuasion: A Cross-Disciplinary Analysis of Math Students' Writing." *Across the Disciplines*, vol. 8, no. 1, 2011, https://wac.colostate.edu/docs/atd/articles/bahlsetal2011.pdf.

Balgopal, Meena M., Alison M. Wallace, and Steven Dahlberg. "Writing to Learn Ecology: A Study of Three Populations of College Students." *Environmental Education Research*, vol. 18, no. 1, 2012, pp. 67–90.

Bean, John C., and Dan Melzer. *Engaging Ideas: The Professor's Guide to Integrating Writing, Critical Thinking, and Active Learning in the Classroom.* Jossey-Bass, 2021.

Bergmann, Linda S., and Janet Zepernick. "Disciplinarity and Transfer: Students' Perceptions of Learning to Write." *Writing Program Administration*, vol. 31, nos. 1–2, 2007, pp. 124–49.

Blaauw-Hara, Mark. "Transfer Theory, Threshold Concepts, and First-Year Composition: Connecting Writing Courses to the Rest of the College." *Teaching English in the Two-Year College*, vol. 41, no. 4, 2014, pp. 354–65.

Boumlik, Habiba, Reem Jaafar, and Ian Alberts. "Women in STEM: A Civic Issue with an Interdisciplinary Approach." *Science Education and Civic Engagement*, vol. 8, no. 1, 2016, pp. 66–88.

Bunch, George C. "Preparing the 'New Mainstream' for College and Careers: Academic and Professional Metagenres in Community Colleges." *Teaching English in the Two-Year College*, vol. 47, no. 2, 2019, pp. 168–94.

Bunch, George C., Heather Schlaman, Nora Lang, and Kylie Kenner. "'Sometimes I Do Not Understand Exactly Where the Difficulties Are for My Students': Language, Literacy, and the New Mainstream in Community Colleges." *Community College Review*, vol. 48, no. 3, 2020, pp. 303–29.

Carroll, Julia, and Helene Dunkelblau. "Preparing ESL Students for 'Real' College Writing: A Glimpse of Common Writing Tasks ESL Students Encounter at One Community College." *Teaching English in the Two-Year College*, vol. 38, no. 3, 2011, pp. 271–81.

Driscoll, Dana Lynn, Joseph Paszek, Gwen Gorzelsky, Carol L. Hayes, and Edmund Jones. "Genre Knowledge and Writing Development: Results from the Writing Transfer Project." *Written Communication*, vol. 37, no. 1, 2020, pp. 69–103.

Dryer, Dylan B. "Scaling Writing Ability: A Corpus-Driven Inquiry." *Written Communication*, vol. 30, no. 1, 2013, pp. 3–35.

Estrada, Samantha. "Drawing Normal Curves: A Visual Analysis of Feedback in Writing-to-Learn Assignments in an Introductory Statistics Course for Community College Students." *The Qualitative Report*, vol. 25, no. 12, 2020, pp. 4423–46.

Fallon, Dianne, Cindy J. Lahar, and David Susman. "Taking the High Road to Transfer: Building Bridges between English and Psychology." *Teaching English in the Two-Year College*, vol. 37, no. 1, 2009, pp. 41–55.

Faulkner, Melissa. "Remediating Remediation: From Basic Writing to Writing across the Curriculum." *CEA Forum*, vol. 42, no. 2, 2013, pp. 45–60.

Fulkerson, Richard. "Composition at the Turn of the Twenty-First Century." *College Composition and Communication*, vol. 56, no. 4, 2005, pp. 654–87.

Hilberg, Jaclyn. "Teaching toward Reading Transfer in Open-Access Contexts: Framing Strategic Reading as a Transferable Skill." *Teaching English in the Two-Year College*, vol. 50, no. 2, 2022, pp. 132–45.

James, Mark Andrew. "The Influence of Perceptions of Task Similarity/Difference on Learning Transfer in Second Language Writing." *Written Communication*, vol. 25, no. 1, 2008, pp. 76–103.

Jarratt, Susan C., Katherine Mack, Alexandra Sartor, and Shevaun E. Watson. "Pedagogical Memory: Writing, Mapping, Translating." *WPA: Writing Program Administration*, vol. 33, nos. 1–2, 2009, pp. 46–73.

Johns, Ann M. "Genre Awareness for the Novice Academic Student: An Ongoing Quest." *Language Teaching*, vol. 41, no. 2, 2008, pp. 237–52.

Kim, Dave, and Wendy M. Olson. "Using a Transfer-Focused Writing Pedagogy to Improve Undergraduates' Lab Report Writing in Gateway Engineering Laboratory Courses." *IEEE Transactions on Professional Communication*, vol. 63, no. 1, 2020, pp. 64–84.

Kim, Jihyun, Christopher Roth, and Sheng Zhang. "Research in the Classroom: Introducing Nanomaterials at a Two-Year College." *International Journal of Research in STEM Education*, vol. 2, no. 2, 2020, pp. 107-13.

Kim, Miseon, Mercedes Franco, and Dugwon Seo. "Implementing Information Literacy (IL) into Stem Writing Courses: Effect of IL Instruction on Students' Writing Projects at an Urban Community College." *Issues in Science and Technology Librarianship*, vol. 94, 2020.

Lee, Joseph J., and Lydia Deakin. "Interactions in L1 and L2 Undergraduate Student Writing: Interactional Metadiscourse in Successful and Less-Successful Argumentative Essays." *Journal of Second Language Writing*, vol. 33, 2016, pp. 21–34.

Martin, Thomas K. *A Study of the Relationship between ENGL1301 and Student Performance in Intensive Writing Courses*, Institutional Research Office, Collin County Community College District, 2009. www.texasair.org/conference/2010/Presentations/B6_ENGL1301_Impact_on_Intensive_Writing.pdf.

Miller, Ryan T., and Silvia Pessoa. "'Where's Your Thesis Statement and What Happened to Your Topic Sentences?': Identifying Organizational Challenges in Undergraduate Student Argumentative Writing." *TESOL Journal*, vol. 7, no. 4, 2016, pp. 847–73.

Miller, Ryan T., Thomas D. Mitchell, and Silvia Pessoa. "Valued Voices: Students' Use of Engagement in Argumentative History Writing." *Linguistics and Education*, vol. 28, 2014, pp. 107–20.

Moore, Jessie. "Mapping the Questions: The State of Writing-Related Transfer Research." *Composition Forum,* vol. 26, 2012.

Nazzal, Jane S., Carol Booth Olson, and Huy Q. Chung. "Differences in Academic Writing across Four Levels of Community College Composition Courses." *Teaching English in the Two-Year College*, vol. 47, no. 3, 2020, pp. 263–96.

Negretti, Raffaella. "Metacognition in Student Academic Writing: A Longitudinal Study of Metacognitive Awareness and Its Relation to Task Perception, Self-Regulation, and Evaluation of Performance." *Written Communication*, vol. 29, no. 2, 2012, pp. 142–79.

Nelms, Gerald, and Ronda Leathers Dively. "Perceived Roadblocks to Transferring Knowledge from First-Year Composition to Writing-Intensive Major Courses: A Pilot Study." *WPA: Writing Program Administration*, vol. 31, nos. 1–2, 2007, pp. 214–40.

Pacello, James. "Developmental Writing and Transfer: Examining Student Perceptions." *Journal of Developmental Education*, vol. 42, no. 3, 2019, pp. 10–17.

Perin, Dolores. "Teaching Academically Underprepared Students in Community Colleges." *Understanding Community Colleges*, edited by John S. Levin and Susan T. Kater, Routledge, 2018, pp. 135–58.

Perrotta, Katherine. "Bringing History to Life: A Study on the Implementation of an Oral History Research Project as a High-Impact Practice in Undergraduate History Courses." *Social Studies*, vol. 110, no. 6, 2019, pp. 267–80.

Rosas Alquicira, Edgar F., Laura Guertin, Sean Tvelia, Peter J. Berquist, and M. W. Cole. "Undergraduate Research at Community Colleges: A Pathway to Achieve Student, Faculty, and Institutional Success." *New Directions for Community Colleges*, vol. 2022, no. 199, 2022, pp. 63–75.

Schrynemakers, Ilse, Cary Lane, Ian Beckford, and Miseon Kim. "College Readiness in Post-Remedial Academia: Faculty Observations from Three Urban Community Colleges." *Community College Enterprise*, vol. 25, no. 1, 2019, pp. 10–31.

Shaver, Lisa. "Eliminating the Shell Game: Using Writing-Assignment Names to Integrate Disciplinary Learning." *Journal of Business and Technical Communication*, vol. 21, no. 1, 2007, pp. 74–90.

Sommers, Nancy, and Laura Saltz. "The Novice as Expert: Writing the Freshman Year." *College Composition and Communication,* vol. 56, no. 1, 2004, pp. 124–49.

Thonney, Teresa. "Analyzing the Vocabulary Demands of Introductory College Textbooks." *The American Biology Teacher*, vol. 78, no. 5, 2016, pp. 389–95.

—. "'At First I Thought . . . But I Don't Know for Sure': The Use of First Person Pronouns in the Academic Writing of Novices." *Across the Disciplines*, vol. 10, no. 1, 2013.

—. "What Community College Instructors Think about Student Writing: Results of a National Survey about Writing across the Curriculum." *College Teaching*, vol. 72, no. 4, 2023, pp. 358–68.

Tila, Dorina. "Writing across the Curriculum (WAC) Assignment in Macroeconomics." *Prompt: A Journal of Academic Writing Assignments*, vol. 6, no. 2, 2022, pp. 122–33.

Tinberg, Howard. "Reconsidering Transfer Knowledge at the Community College: Challenges and Opportunities." *Teaching English in the Two-Year College*, vol. 43, no. 1, 2015, pp. 7–31.

Tinberg, Howard, and Jean-Paul Nadeau. *The Community College Writer: Exceeding Expectations*. Southern Illinois UP, 2010.

Traver, Amy E. "How Do We Integrate Students' Vocational Goals into Introduction to Sociology Curricula, and What Are the Effects of Doing So?" *Teaching Sociology*, vol. 44, no. 4, 2016, pp. 287–95.

Uccelli, Paola, Christina L. Dobbs, and Jessica Scott. "Mastering Academic Language: Organization and Stance in the Persuasive Writing of High School Students." *Written Communication*, vol. 30, no. 1, 2013, pp. 36–62.

Varelas, Antonios, Kate S. Wolfe, and Ernest Ialongo. "Building a Better Student: Developing Critical Thinking and Writing in the Community College from Freshman Semester to Graduation." *Community College Enterprise*, vol. 21, no. 2, 2015, pp. 76–92.

Wandersee, James H., Renee M. Clary, and Sandra M. Guzman. "A Writing Template for Probing Students' Botanical Sense of Place." *American Biology Teacher*, vol. 68, no. 7, 2006, pp. 419–22.

Wardle, Elizabeth. "Understanding 'Transfer' from FYC: Preliminary Results of a Longitudinal Study." *WPA: Writing Program Administration*, vol. 31, nos. 1–2, 2007, pp. 65–85.

Worden-Chambers, Dorothy, and Ashley S. Montgomery. "How Writing Teachers' Beliefs about Learning Transfer Impact Their Teaching Practices: A Case from L2 Academic Writing." *WPA: Writing Program Administration*, vol. 46, no. 1, 2022, pp. 117–36.

Yancey, Kathleen Blake, Liane Robertson, and Kara Taczak. *Writing across Contexts: Transfer, Composition, and Sites of Writing*. Utah State UP, 2014.

Teresa Thonney is emeritus professor of English at Columbia Basin College. Her writing and research interests include writing across the curriculum and writing in the disciplines.

Book Reviews

A Transdisciplinary Approach to Writing Knowledge Transfer: Applications in Teaching and Research

Hunter Little

Nowacek, Rebecca S., Rebecca Lorimer Leonard, and Angela Rounsaville. *Writing Knowledge Transfer: Theory, Research, and Pedagogy*. Parlor Press; The WAC Clearinghouse, 2024. 454 pages.

Implicitly or explicitly, the existence of first-year writing (FYW) courses has been, in part, dependent on claims about the generalizability of writing knowledge and its potential to be transferred—whether it can be adopted and adapted appropriately for use in students' academic and professional lives. While writing studies scholars' reinforcement of and evidence that transfer does and can occur under certain conditions has worked to address what Rebecca S. Nowacek in 2011 described as a prevalent disbelief in generalizable utility that threatened the "abolition" of FYW courses (12), transfer continues to be a major concern for writing studies, be that in "the quiet presence of transfer" in WAC/WID (Nowacek, Lorimer Leonard, and Rounsaville 208) or in studies and courses explicitly designed through transfer theory and principles. The question of writing knowledge transfer is imperative for the work of WPAs as they develop FYW curricula, instructor training programs and support resources, and WAC/WID courses as well as gauge their programs' effectiveness and make pitches regarding program funding. However, writing studies scholars have been limited by the lack of transdisciplinarity in our methods for supporting and studying transfer. And, in terms of program building and pedagogical applications of transfer research, WPAs and writing instructors have had limited access to comprehensive transdisciplinary resources for what has been learned from transfer research.

In *Writing Knowledge Transfer: Theory, Research, and Pedagogy*, Rebecca S. Nowacek, Rebecca Lorimer Leonard, and Angela Rounsaville offer a much-needed synthesis in the field of writing studies that combines transfer research from 596 articles and 138 books across various disciplines (315). They take a transdisciplinary approach which emphasizes how the siloing of disciplines restricts what and how we can know about transfer and limits possibilities for our students to transfer writing knowledge, hoping to "reposition writing studies at the intersection of multiple transfer research strands" (315). Through their forging of cross-disciplinary connections, they cover a lot of ground, compiling a thorough text that captures the true complexity of transfer as a phenomenon in all areas of learning. The authors take a distant to local approach to expand transfer through already-established lines of thought in other fields by introducing those further from writing studies before delving into conversations more closely linked to writing studies. They first present their approach, goals, and overview of the book in chapter 1, "Introduction," problematizing the "carry" metaphor that has historically been adopted by transfer scholars. In chapter 2, "Cognitive Psychology and Situated Learning: Foundational Research on Transfer of Learning," they bridge writing studies' transfer research and transfer's early history in psychology and education to highlight the necessity of both individual and contextual foci in transfer research. This necessity is further supported in chapter 3, "Transfer of Training and Knowledge Management: Research from Industrial Psychology, Human Resources, and Management," where they review work on the training of individuals, the impact of relationships and workplace environments, and the value of error in transfer processes. In chapter 4, "Transfer in Sports, Medical, Aviation, and Military Training," we learn about the role of the body's memory in supporting transfer as these disciplines emphasize "the body and the body's relationship to cognition and context" (91) through attention to situated learning and contextual fidelity.

Shifting toward those disciplines positioned closer to writing studies, chapter 5, "Transfer Implications from Sociocultural and Sociohistorical Literacy Studies," presents concerns about how transfer should be understood as intertwined with various systems of power that reserve transfer benefits for students whose home and cultural experiences align with school practices and values (113–14) which underscores a persistent goal in writing studies to value students' multiliteracies. Second language writing becomes a focal point in chapter 6, "Research on Transfer in Studies of Second Language Writing," where language is presented as one of the "dynamic factors" (138) of transfer that requires us to address how writing knowledge moves among contexts and languages (131). The authors also pair this discussion with highlights on the positive outcomes that result from genre-based writing instruction. Chapter 7, "Transfer in First-Year Writing," and chapter 8, "Infrastructure for the Transfer of Writing Knowledge: Writing Across the Curriculum and Writing in the Disciplines," cover transfer's existing role in writing studies, including concerns with prior knowledge, genre, and dispositions. Chapter 8, in particular, traces how WAC/WID are shaped by transfer principles through their focus on disciplinary writing tasks that guide students toward connections across fields.

Such courses support students' ability to transfer and our ability to support transfer through exposure to specific genres and situations students might encounter later (207). Writing centers' role in the transfer of writing knowledge is discussed in chapter 9, "Writing Centers: An Infrastructural Hub for Transfer," emphasizing the need for tutors to learn transfer and genre theories to better benefit students writing in other disciplines. Chapter 10, "Writing across Contexts: From School to Work and Beyond," further centers situated learning through the lens of workplace preparation and reinforces the fact that students' activity systems are constantly interlocking and overlapping to contribute to each transfer act, which should prevent us from drawing too stiff a boundary between school and work contexts.

As a transfer scholar myself, this book reads in part as a review on traditional studies of transfer, including connections to the work of notable transfer scholars, such as David Perkins and Gavriel Salomon; Nowacek; John D. Bransford and Daniel L. Schwartz; Dana Lynn Driscoll; Mary Jo Reiff and Anis Bawarshi; Elizabeth Wardle; Kathleen Blake Yancey, Liane Robertson, and Kara Taczak; and Edward L. Thorndike and Robert S. Woodworth. However, the book is refreshing and stimulating as Nowacek, Lorimer Leonard, and Rounsaville's comprehensive synthesis provides relief and generates excitement about the many possibilities we can imagine through the unity of multiple disciplines invested in a similar interest. Beyond giving hope and broader range to those already invested in transfer research, this text is accessible for those with any research focus and at any stage of their academic career, while synthesizing knowledge in ways that will be readily applicable for WPAs. For writing studies readers who do not define themselves as transfer scholars, the book will prove useful in showcasing the universality of transfer in our field, whether they work in writing centers, second language writing, teacher education, literacy studies, FYW, or lead writing programs. Through their self-proclaimed meta-approach, Nowacek, Lorimer Leonard, and Rounsaville expect action to result from one's reading of this text, making it both a toolbox and a model for supporting the transfer of learning as they make connections between fields for us, supporting our own transfer of knowledge to inspire all scholars and instructors in writing studies to adopt and use said knowledge.

Such an adoption is made possible through the accessible nature of the text. Each chapter begins with an outline of the usefulness of transfer work in other fields for supporting writing knowledge transfer. This makes the necessity of our investment immediately apparent and cues and primes us for how we might employ this initial learning in our research and teaching. They are transparent about their "'synthesis' approach" and explain the purposeful organization of the chapters, for example, that the sections in chapter 8 are "organized by researchers' common problems or questions about the transfer of writing knowledge in WAC/WID" (209). This approach results in an abundance of transfer research examples that act as evidence for the subsequent claims about their application in writing studies, such as in their review of Dan Fraizer's approach to departmental communication, which presents a "dialogic model that promotes faculty awareness of transfer" by fostering ongoing conversations about how to apply disciplinary threshold concepts (225). As the authors move through the sections, they review the literature intentionally and propose clear directions of thought and action; their tone is never demanding but welcoming, asking us to further engage our creative and critical capacities to unfold greater possibilities for writing and transfer studies and, thus, our students while leaving space for theories to be left up for debate in their juxtaposition of transfer findings. For example, in chapter 4 they write, "This work might ask us to consider how disaggregating features of writing from their genres and communities does not necessarily disrupt or support the ways writers have deeply internalized when and how to use certain skills and strategies over others" (92). Moreover, the sections are productively succinct and outlined within the table of contents for easy navigation based on the interests and goals of the reader. All of the chapters' concluding sections explain what has been discussed and why, providing implications for writing studies—for example, in "Methodological Implications from Literacy Studies" (122), "Curricular Recommendations and Innovations for Transfer in First-Year Writing" (193), and "Conclusion and Avenues for Further Inquiry in Writing Studies" (104).

Writing Knowledge Transfer's discipline-specific chapters are followed by chapter 11, "Conclusion: Transfer and Transdisciplinarity in Five Themes," which is solely devoted to outlining five key transdisciplinary themes within the research—individuality, intentionality, fidelity, directionality, and simultaneity—which arose out of the authors' composition of the volume and are drawn from the scholarship reviewed therein. These themes are presented as "pathways" and "entry points into new frames" for approaching "transfer of writing-related knowledge and activity" along with examples of how each theme might manifest in writing studies research and praxis (315). Each theme speaks either to transfer studies' units of analysis, central questions, contexts or relations, spatiotemporal elements, or the complexity of an individual transfer act and together guide us toward "future frames" for harnessing the transformative potential of a transdisciplinary approach to writing transfer research and instruction. In addition, they provide a glossary that is helpful for familiarizing oneself with some of the highly theoretical content and which links such content to its respective scholars, some of which are selected for presentation in an annotated bibliography to further inspire engagement with transfer research.

Through their posing of productive challenges, Nowacek, Lorimer Leonard, and Rounsaville build a text that can be used by WPAs in a variety of ways and within a range of contexts. They might, for instance, use this text to guide their own research and instruction whether they are a long-time transfer scholar or using the book to familiarize themselves with transfer key terms and studies. The authors also indicate the necessity of greater attention to transfer in our curricular design for "intentionally making writing knowledge transparent, explicit, and relevant to students' lives" (210), since "explicit instruction of disciplinary writing values, beliefs, genres, expectations, and practices is essential to transfer" (221). This explicit instruction could be paired with emphasis on peer-to-peer interaction and instructor support and feedback (62), which respond to both the social and individual elements that contribute to the success of transfer rather than "the ways transfer research has consolidated around individuals" (316) since "individual characteristics exist in a dynamic relationship with social contexts for learning" (59).

A central argument within these lines that might particularly resonate with WPAs is that teacher training needs to more purposefully teach transfer research and principles. At many universities, FYW courses are taught by graduate student instructors making the pedagogical implications and approaches presented in chapter 7 an important point of focus for not only readers in transfer studies and WPAs, but also individuals new to teaching writing (e.g., 193–95). This book deserves space within teacher training to help instructors design courses that support goals and outcomes consistent with theories of writing knowledge transfer and convey writing tasks' relevance to students. Using this text to inform teacher training programs also represents its utility in producing and revising course learning outcomes that are more explicitly informed by transdisciplinary transfer principles. Since they consistently refer to preceding and succeeding chapters throughout, each can be read alone or in varied combinations for new and/or more experienced instructors.

In the section "Teacher Knowledge about Disciplinary Writing Transfer" in chapter 8, the authors argue for more consistent transdisciplinary work among instructors, stating "instructors across programs and departments need a shared vocabulary about writing to dismantle . . . roadblocks to transfer" and suggest "venues like WAC/WID workshops to support increased communication and interdisciplinary exchange around writing concepts, skills, genres, and student attitudes" (223). Thus, this text can be used as justification for greater investment in disciplinary writing courses and programs and, with the "guiding assumption that the authenticity of the workplace helps to facilitate the transfer of learning from school to work" (302), WPAs are called to create more opportunities for students to participate in service and immersive learning, classroom-based interactions, and workplace-based internships that are more authentic.

What particularly struck me as both a transfer and disability studies scholar was the emphasis on embodied cognition in chapter 4. In their conclusion, Nowacek, Lorimer Leonard, and Rounsaville emphasize how "the body is always active and present in learning" (320) and it is therefore "a crucial element of cognition" (321). Because memories are lived in the body, how we engage with objects, ideas, and concepts (i.e., writing) makes transfer physical as well. Historically, high-road and far-reaching forms of transfer have been valorized (35), leaving more "automatic, embodied, and non-verbalized forms of transfer" (88) to go undervalued or worse, ignored or labeled as "negative" transfer. Thus, we need to better value low-road or automatized transfer rather than casting our attention solely toward high-road transfer. For example, in "medical education, so-called high-road transfer must be coupled with low-road transfer for quick thinking and automaticity of action" (96–97), and in cognitive psychology, this concept is called dual processing: the stimulation of (a) unconscious or automatic transfer and (b) deliberate or conscious transfer (33). This push toward countering traditional views of transfer as always intentional also echoes Nowacek's argument in *Agents of Integration: Understanding Transfer as a Rhetorical Act* that there is no negative transfer but "unexpected" transfer that does not align with what instructors and researchers anticipate. To me, attention to the body's role in writing could be a call for WPAs to continue advocating for multimodal-specific courses and encouraging instructors to assign multimodal and embodied forms of composing that emphasize the body as part of the process. This could be an opportunity to provide instructors models for metacognitive tasks that involve reflections on students' movement, location, and affect as they complete an assignment. Although the authors inspire us to opt for "more complex and dynamic" transfer models (334) through their fronting of the bodymind connection and argue for "a transfer curriculum that centers students' histories, languages, and identities in ways that fully integrate social and linguistic justice in the aims and methods of the course" (199), they do not delve into conversations about how disability could impact transfer of learning. The idea that disability is potentiating for challenging traditional views of writing and writing practices, for example, remains an area worth further exploring and could guide WPAs toward even more accessibility-informed standards for teaching and assessing writing.

In short, Nowacek, Lorimer Leonard, and Rounsaville's *Writing Knowledge Transfer* demonstrates that a transdisciplinary emphasis in transfer studies, writing studies, and writing program administration is essential since we can become better instructors and researchers by adopting and expanding on knowledge about transfer from other fields. This book is what we need now when transfer is becoming more central to writing studies as well as when new and conflicting perspectives on transfer are arising. It asks writing studies scholars to slow down (much in the way we need students to for mindful abstraction) and embrace those connections between disciplines. For me, *Writing Knowledge Transfer* came at a time when transdisciplinarity and other unifying initiatives and perspectives are prevalent and is beneficial for what it both explicitly and implicitly suggests about transfer research in writing studies, making a compelling case that, because transfer is for everyone, this book is for everyone.

Works Cited

Bransford, John D. and Daniel L. Schwartz. "Rethinking Transfer: A Simple Proposal with Multiple Implications." *Review of Research in Education*, vol. 24, no. 1, 1999, pp. 61–100, https://doi.org/10.3102/0091732X024001061.

Driscoll, Dana Lynn. "Building Connections and Transferring Knowledge: The Benefits of a Peer Tutoring Course Beyond the Writing Center." *The Writing Center Journal*, vol. 35, no. 1, 2015, pp. 153–181, https://www.jstor.org/stable/43673622.

Fraizer, Dan. "Towards a Model of Building Writing Transfer Awareness Across the Curriculum." *Composition Forum*, vol. 38 (Spring), 2018, https://www.compositionforum.com/issue/38/transfer-awareness.php.

Nowacek, Rebecca S. *Agents of Integration: Understanding Transfer as a Rhetorical Act*. Southern Illinois University Press, 2011.

Nowacek, Rebecca S., Rebecca Lorimer Leonard, and Angela Rounsaville. *Writing Knowledge Transfer: Theory, Research, Pedagogy*. Parlor Press; The WAC Clearinghouse, 2024.

Perkins, David and Gavriel Salomon. "Are Cognitive Skills Context-Bound?" *Educational Researcher*, vol. 18, no. 1, 1989, pp. 16–25, https://www.jstor.org/stable/1176006.

Perkins, David and Gavriel Salomon. "Knowledge to Go: A Motivational and Dispositional View of Transfer." *Educational Psychologist*, vol. 47, no. 3, 2012, pp. 248–258, https://doi.org/10.1080/00461520.2012.693354.

Reiff, Mary Jo and Anis Bawarshi. "Tracing Discursive Resources: How Students Use Prior Genre Knowledge to Negotiate New Writing Contexts in First-Year Composition." *Written Communication*, vol. 28, no. 3, 2011, pp. 312–337, https://doi.org/10.1177/0741088311410183.

Thorndike, Edward L. and Robert S. Woodworth. "The Influence of Improvement in One Mental Function Upon the Efficiency of Other Functions. (I)."

Psychological Review, vol. 8, no. 3, 1901, pp. 247-61, https://psycnet.apa.org/doi/10.1037/h0074898.

Wardle, Elizabeth. "Understanding 'transfer' from FYC: Preliminary Results of a Longitudinal Study." *WPA: Writing Program Administration*, vol. 31, no. 1–2, 2007, pp. 65–85, http://associationdatabase.co/archives/31n1-2/31n1-2wardle.pdf.

Yancey, Kathleen Blake, Liane Robertson, and Kara Taczak. *Writing Across Contexts: Transfer, Composition, and Sites of Writing*. Utah State University Press, 2014.

Hunter Little is a fifth-year PhD candidate in the Department of English at the University of Washington Seattle. Proximal to defense, Hunter's dissertation research forges connections between the fields of disability studies, writing studies, and knowledge transfer studies. She is interested in using knowledge transfer principles to promote disability literacy across campus and the uptake and adaptation of knowledge about mental disability. Little currently teaches interdisciplinary writing courses within UW's Program in Writing Across Campus.

Review of *Two-Year College Writing Studies*

Donny Penner

Jensen, Darin, and Brett Griffiths. *Two-Year College Writing Studies: Rationale and Praxis for Just Teaching.* Utah State UP, 2023. 200 pages.

In *Two-Year College Writing Studies*, Darin Jensen and Brett Griffiths have curated a collection of essays they describe as "a love letter to the two-year college as an ideal" (22). Its authors write about history, pedagogy, theory, and administration, all within the unique contexts of two-year colleges. It's written for stakeholders at those institutions, and as a writing teacher at a rural community college, I am Jensen and Griffith's target audience. However, this book deserves a wider readership among our profession because its contents offer essential contributions to writing studies' ongoing conversations about labor, professionalization, and linguistic justice. I cannot, of course, fairly review a love letter written for me or the ideals I share with the authors, but I will describe its contents with joy and, I hope, convey some of the lessons that teachers working with America's most diverse writing community hope to share with peers who would listen.

For those unfamiliar with composition at two-year colleges, *Two-Year College Writing Studies* is a good introduction. The authors take care to describe the unique context in which their contributors' knowledge is produced, and make substantial efforts to translate the often informal work of two-year college teacher-scholars into robust theory and praxis. The task is formidable. It's well known that the majority of community colleges don't have formal writing program administrators or research demands, despite the fact that their faculty teach the majority of first-year writing classes in the United States. It's reasonable to say they know the most about teaching "basic" writers and running first-year writing programs for diverse populations. However, they are not central to conversations about either. One need only browse reading lists in most graduate programs to see it. Indeed, this disparity between the labor and scholarship about the labor is a visceral tension throughout the collection. The rationale for *Two-Year College Writing Studies*, from its sober voice, to its text selection, to its organization, all feels informed, haunted even, by the depreciated status of the two-year college, its student populations, its faculty, and their expertise. In this sense, the collection fills a gap in writing studies canon. It acts as "a set of counternarratives threading through our discipline and cuffing at the margins of our profession" (162), making an argument that two-year college teacher-scholars are and always have been a cornerstone for the writing studies field.

Two-Year College Writing Studies isn't the first collection to frame the work and scholarship of two-year college instructors as central to larger disciplinary conversations. It's a continuation of Mark Reynold's and Sylvia Holladay-Hicks's collection *The Profession of English in the Two-year College*, Patrick Sullivan and Christie Toth's T*eaching Composition at the Two-Year College*, and dozens of other essays, published primarily in *Teaching English at the Two-Year College*. Reynolds writes the book's foreword, and all of the contributing essayists have published similar work before. In fact, faculty at two-year colleges have vied for a place in disciplinary conversations since their inception more than a century ago. Given the historical context and exigence of the collection, it emanates an ethos of de-centering knowledge that can be felt most vividly by the teachers who live and work in the spaces Griffiths and Jensen describe. Overall, the book lingers on context and conditions. In their own words, the collection "seeks to create a space that allows the most diverse of institutions . . . to be examined so our practices and selves can serve our students and the institutions' democratic potential" (22).

The book contains seven essays, bookended by an introduction and afterword by the editors. As a body of work, its contents begin by establishing historical context. Patrick Sullivan, a household name in two-year college scholarship, uses the first essay to paint two-year colleges as social justice institutions that struggle to fulfill their promise. Sullivan builds on the 1947 Truman Commission on Higher Education to argue that the establishment of a robust and comprehensive community college system in the United States was an "extraordinary historical moment" (27) in American democracy. He further argues that civil rights activism in the 1960's and 70's by African American and Latinx activists led to federally (well-) funded community colleges in the United States. Sullivan's history establishes a secondary argument: that community colleges have fallen short of delivering equitable and accessible education. Structural racism still harms outcomes for marginalized student populations, neoliberal ideology diminishes working conditions for teachers, equitable assessment remains largely out of reach at institutions with excessive administrative oversight, and the same austerity that has affected most institutions of higher learning has been especially hard on community colleges. Sullivan's history of the community college is, like all history, highly rhetorical. It recalls a community college golden age that may not have existed. But he is right about the distinct position community colleges and their stakeholders find themselves in, and paints a vivid picture for fellow writing teachers at other institutions.

The next three essays highlight several examples of classroom pedagogy used to effectively teach in the historical contexts summarized by Sullivan, contexts where students are often marginalized and provided with inadequate resources to meet academic expectations. In the first, Bernice Olivas asks how the social justice mission of the community college can be translated to praxis in the classroom. She astutely observes that one of the most pressing challenges for community college students is their alienation from performing academic identities, of not feeling like "college students." To address the issue, Olivas argues that the writing teacher must also be an identity agent. She grounds this practice in identity control theory (ICT), and adopts a pedagogy focused on self-reflection, separation of judgment and observation, the use of dialogue, and a focus on building alliances and common ground with students. Her courses ask students to examine writing identities and misconceptions, privilege, marginalization, and the ways college writing might affect them. It's not uncommon for first-year writing courses to directly address the student's writerly identity, but in Olivas's case, and for all community college teachers, identity agency directly affects student success. That is, addressing academic identity must accompany cultural identity and writerly identity. Her work reminds us that many community college students face the additional challenge of cultivating an academic self before they can undertake the rigorous work expected of them in higher education. Given this challenge, the composition teacher bears the responsibility of preparing students for more than writing—they are identity agents for their students.

In a similar vein, Emily K. Suh's contribution to the collection addresses the ways in which instructors are ineffective identity agents. Using Bourdieu's concept of *symbolic capital*, i.e. socially assigned resources and experiences with nonmonetary value (62), she posits that teachers sometimes fall short of helping students translate the assets they bring with them to college into academic success. Her essay employs two case studies from immigrant students who relied on cultural norms and personal circumstances to navigate college in the absence of traditional academic skillsets. Ultimately, the students were limited by relying only on their prior knowledge and experience because teachers failed to create collaborative plans that could help the students utilize their symbolic capital in the context of academic expectations. Suh's case studies are uncomfortable to read because, for most two-year college writing teachers, they are all too common. Fortunately, she offers optimism in the form of lessons learned that readers might use to bridge the gap between symbolic capital and academic literacy. First, says Suh, teachers must recognize the symbolic capital that their students possess. Next, they must help them distinguish between prior knowledge and aspirational identities. Finally, teachers must collaborate with students to make meaning from their experiences within an institutional context (74).

In the next essay, Jamila M. Kareem applies critical race theory (CRT) to composition studies' "critically conscious practices" (79). She exposes embedded racial ideologies and offers a way forward for a more raciolinguistically just method of teaching composition, with lists of exercises, readings, and module designs. Kareem argues that the CCCC *Students' Right to Their Own Language* (SRTOL) fails to go far enough to disrupt dominant raciolinguistic narratives and images. Similarly, she critiques the CCCC *Statement on Second Language Writing and Multilingual Writers* (SOSL), arguing that while it does expose students to criticisms of raciolinguistic attitudes, it does not encourage students to use their own language practices in critical reflection. Kareem looks most favorably at the CCCC 2020 *This Ain't Another Statement! This is a DEMAND for Black Linguistic Justice!* She argues that where others have fallen short, the document has the potential to promote systematic change among administrators, especially at two-year college institutions. Kareem then offers more linguistically equitable instructional practices to the reader. These include an "academic cultural language statement" that promises students she will not assess non-dominant English differently than standard English, so long as they are aware of the linguistic, grammatical, and rhetorical effects of their work. She also teaches multiple raciolinguistic rhetorical traditions, including African American, Latinx, and Indigenous, and western rhetorical practices. Lastly, she assigns readings on language ideology and myth. Kareem's suggestions imagine a richer and more translingual approach to writing. Her comparative rhetorical model should prove especially useful for first-year writing teachers, especially those without composition training, because it escapes the typical Aristotelian box consisting of logos, ethos, pathos, and the rhetorical situation.

Three concluding essays consider how the unique positions of community college writing programs and/or departments influence decisions at the programmatic level. Rhonda Grego thinks about the ways that departmental administrators can professionally develop their faculty and equitably assess student work within thirdspaces, or knowledge making spaces distinct from formal institutional and classroom activity. As she transitioned from instructor to Dean of Humanities at her institution, Grego quickly recognized that she needed to satisfy institutional assessment standards without imposing de-professionalizing assessment rubrics on her faculty. Given the limitations for professional development at her institution, she utilized writing studio models and individualized assessment journals to provide students and faculty with a place both outside the classroom and beyond the confines of institutional structure in which to consciously reflect on their own practices. Thirdspace thinking seems especially important for writing departments at community colleges and institutions who cannot always provide adequate resources (time, space, funding) for faculty to cultivate professional identities.

In their essay "The Painful Eagerness of Unfed Hope," Kirsten Higgins, Anthony Warnke, and Jake Frye resist what they call "good enough" assessment practices—or the mentality of meeting minimum institutional mandates as a response to working in austere conditions. They argue that following a "good-enough" schema leads to reification of the status quo. Despite noble intentions, argue the authors, when faculty entertain assessment practices that only meet minimum requirements, they ultimately "structure in and perpetuate inequities that undermine our students and profession" (129). For Higgins, Warnke, and Frye, the status quo equates to ineffective and unethical assessment grounded in ideologies that seek to improve student success by quantifying their performance. Normative assessment is, in their words, a neoliberal anxiety that is "an outcome assessment's pathology even as it purports to be its cure" (132). As an alternative to the "good enough" mentality, the authors suggest dispositions of disruption and rhetorical attunement. Disposition entails professional engagement with disciplinary traditions in order to critically assess and denormalize the status quo. Rhetorical attunement involves a conscious effort of listening, observing, and "paying attention to what often goes overlooked or undervalued in our institutions" (136). They conclude by offering explanations for how this might be put into practice. Higgins, Warnke, and Frye propose that all assessments be grounded in ecological snapshots of student demographics, that faculty take a translingual approach to students' language goals, and for assessors to reorient their understanding of language as a multiplicity of practices. The chapter marks an ideal rather than a study, but it's one that many readers who may feel stuck in the mud with assessment may find encouraging. Their work imagines what a future in writing assessment could look like. While they admit that their solutions may not be possible in all institutions, the essay creates a powerful primer for critical reform.

Yet, the editors understand that even the best ideas face limitations beyond faculty members' control. In the collection's final essay, Joanne Baird Giordano and Holly Hassel describe their successful implementation of a faculty and discipline-based writing program, only to have it gutted when their state legislature decided to consolidate higher education and place all community colleges under university control. Giordano and Hassel remind the reader that community colleges are particularly susceptible to state and national political mandates, and must always respond to whichever direction political winds blow. This sensitivity to political whims requires college faculty to be activists themselves, argue the authors. However, they add that some issues faculty face cannot be addressed with individual activism, and require strategic organizing at a national level. Ultimately, they advocate for organizations like the Two-Year College English Association (TYCA) as a resource that gives "two-year college faculty the ability to address imposed mandates in ways that can limit harm to teachers, students, and their communities" (158). The essay reminds us that while all community colleges exist in unique ecologies, faculty must engage with larger knowledge networks in order to establish a more robust professional ethos capable of weathering politics that don't always have students' or teachers' best interests in mind.

Two-Year College Writing Studies is only a snapshot of the rich, complex, and century-old profession of two-year college writing instruction. It is a love letter, as Jenson and Griffiths claim, but reads like a disciplinary introduction. Because of this, its 174-page length feels brief, as if each of the essays only scratches the surface of what their authors could provide to a reader. The collection offers resources for two-year college instructors to think about their historical context, how they might address longstanding issues in open-access classrooms, and new ways they might work as disciplinary experts at an administrative level. However, any reader seriously interested in tapping into the body of knowledge two-year college writing studies has cultivated must look beyond. *Two-Year College Writing Studies* is a starting point for academics who want to know more about two-year colleges, and is especially relevant for WPAs at universities and teaching colleges who are increasingly tasked with constructing concurrent enrollment courses, reforming basic writing courses, and addressing diverse classrooms filled with underprepared students. The collection also serves as a reminder of the classroom, administrative and activist possibilities for faculty who already work in those spaces. Its essays provide pathways for disrupting fossilized and harmful assessment and placement practices. It offers guidance on professional development where taken-for-granted resources in other contexts may not be available. Lastly, it offers more equitable, just, and effective possibilities for praxis in the classroom. Jenson and Griffiths' book should be read by anyone who teaches writing, but cannot be taken as a definitive guide. It is only the beginning, and as the authors remind us, the work continues, and the next step begins with the readers.

Works Cited

CCCC Statement on a Student's Right to Their Own Language. CCCC, 1974, cccc. ncte.org/cccc/resources/positions/srtolsummary.

CCCC Statement on Second Language Writing and Multilingual Writers. CCCC, 2020, cccc.ncte.org/cccc/resources/positions/secondlangwriting.

Jensen, Darin, and Brett Griffiths. *Two-Year College Writing Studies: Rationale and Praxis for Just Teaching.* Utah State UP, 2023.

Reynolds, Mark, and Sylvia Holladay-Hicks, editors. *The Profession of English in the Two-year College.* Heinemann, 2005.

Sullivan, Patrick, and Christie Toth, editors. *Teaching Composition at the Two-Year College: Background Readings.* Bedford/St. Martin's, 2016.

This Ain't Another Statement! This is a DEMAND for Black Linguistic Justice! CCCC, 2020, cccc.ncte.org/cccc/demand-for-black-linguistic-justice.

Donny Penner is a full-time instructor of English at Cochise College, a community college in southern Arizona. His office is located approximately one mile from Mexico, which his transborder students refer to as *el otro lado*. He currently serves on the editorial board of *Teaching English in the Two-Year College*, and previously served as the editorial assistant for *The Writing Center Journal*.

Extending an invitation to join the

Council of

Writing Program Administrators

The Council of Writing Program Administrators offers a national network of scholarship and support for leaders of college and university writing programs.

Membership benefits include the following:

- A subscription to *WPA: Writing Program Administration*, a semi-annual refereed journal
- Unrestricted access to journal archives and job boards
- Participation on WPA committees and task forces
- Invitations to the annual WPA Summer Workshops and Conferences
- Invitations to submit papers for sessions that WPA sponsors at MLA and CCCC
- Participation in the WPA Research Grant Program, which distributes several awards, ranging from $1,000 to $2,000
- Invitation to the annual WPA breakfast at CCCC
- Information about the WPA Consultant-Evaluator Service

Membership Rates

- Lifetime Membership GOLD: print journal, conference registration, and membership for life: $3,000
- Lifetime Membership SILVER: print journal and membership for life: $1,500
- Member Level 3 (income over $100,000): $150/year (Green option: $125*)
- Member Level 2 (income $40,000-$100,000): $100/year (Green option: $80*)
- Member Level 1 (income under $40,000): $55/year (Green option: $45*)
- Student Member: $30/year (Green option: $20*)
- Emeritus Member: $30/year (Green option: $20*)
- Institutional Membership (1 print journal to institution and 1 WPA membership, including journal): $250

*Green option - receives digital journal in lieu of print journal

For More Information

Visit us online at http://wpacouncil.org.

PARLOR PRESS
EQUIPMENT FOR LIVING

Now with Parlor Press!

Studies in Rhetorics and Feminism
  New Series Editors: Jessica Enoch and Sharon Yam

Critical Conversations in Higher Education Leadership
  Series Editor: Victor E. Taylor

New Releases

Writing Proposals and Grants 3e by Richard Johnson-Sheehan and Paul Thompson Hunter

Rhetorics of Evidence: Science – Media – Culture edited by edited by Olaf Kramer and Michael Pelzer

Kenneth Burke's Rhetoric of Identification by Tilly Warnock

The Forever Colony by Victor Villanueva

Keywords in Making edited by Jason Tham

Inclusive Aims: Rhetoric's Role in Reproductive Justice edited by Heather Brook Adams and Nancy Myers

Not Playing Around: Feminist and Queer Rhetorics in Videogames by Rebecca Richards

Design for Composition: Inspiration for Creative Visual and Multimodal Projects by Sohui Lee and Russell Carpenter

MLA Mina Shaughnessy Prize and CCCC Best Book Award 2021!

Creole Composition: Academic Writing and Rhetoric in the Anglophone Caribbean, edited by Vivette Milson-Whyte, Raymond Oenbring, and Brianne Jaquette

Check Out Our Website!

Discounts, blog, open access titles, instant downloads, and more.

www.parlorpress.com

CWPA Discount: Use CWPA30 at checkout to receive a 30% discount on all titles not on sale through December 31, 2024.